I'm

And This Is How I See It

I'm Walter Furley And This Is How I See It

compiled by Ric Furley
edited by Ann Marie Evans

How I See it Publishing
Austin, Texas

cover photo by Dick Wittliff Photography
used by permission

cover design by Ann Marie Evans

printed by CreateSpace, An Amazon Company
available from Amazon.com and other retail outlets

Contents

2007

2009

2010

2011

2012

Forward

Ric Furley

My father was Walter Furley, the voice of Corpus Christi, Texas.

His broadcast career lasted more than 50 years, and countless citizens of this sparkling city grew up watching him as news anchor for KZTV. He began that career in the early days of television, and his boss Vann M. Kennedy had very strict rules for his on-air personalities: no editorializing. "Just the plain facts are all you need in a news story." And—the 11th commandment—no chit-chat.

Dad was very proud of his career and immensely respectful of his employer, and he followed these rules, literally to the letter, for all of those decades.

Until now…

Shortly after Dad retired, he began a series of on-air editorials via his KZTV home. These were called "Frankly Furley," and in them he unleashed surprising wit and humor on his beloved listeners. Though short lived, "Frankly Furley" had many fans. After it ended, Dad wrote poems for friends and family, achieved a new wave of fame for the "odes" he wrote for local luminaries, and even masterfully interpreted our own national anthem.

A few years later, Stewart Jacoby of KEDT invited Dad to do a weekly column on public radio. "This is How I See It" was born. Dad loved the freedom he found in doing these editorials, and they helped keep his mind sharp and his wit keen. He wrote and delivered over 200 missives from that date until one month prior to his passing. Almost all of them were done in one take.

All this happened while I was living in Austin, and rarely, if ever, did I get to hear these broadcasts.

Through this book, I get to have a whole new relationship with my father and his memories! I am more than excited to share them with you!

Ric Furley

Summer 2015

Forward

Stewart Jacoby

The request seemed a simple one: "Would you be interested in airing a few commentaries each month on our radio station? You can choose any subject you'd like. And, of course, it will be on a voluntary basis; there will be no salary." It was understood that while the request painted a broad picture of possible subjects, controversial issues would not be tackled on our medium market public radio station.

The request was made to Walter Furley soon after his retirement. And, it would mean that while a major era in his professional life had ended, a new one—with new challenges—would begin. I suppose that I might have found such a task to be a daunting one, but not Walter Furley. Not for a man who was the epitome of the consummate professional, and who had been mentally storing up multitudes of random observations in his razor-sharp mind for most of his life.

In the weeks, months, and years that followed, each commentary would manifest itself as if an inner-thought or simple observation had been waiting patiently in the wings for a chance to take center stage and say, "Hey look at me, I've been here all the time—right under your nose!" Walter Furley's commentaries, "That's The Way I See It" aired two to four times a month for nearly a decade on South Texas Public Radio's KEDT-FM in Corpus Christi, Texas.

By the time the request was made, Furley was enthusiastically ready to accept any opportunity that allowed him to continue exercising his considerable creative talents. We had made the same request of another longtime South Texas journalist, Juliet Wenger. She and Furley would alternate their scheduled commentaries every other week, month-to-month. They had been friends as well as colleagues over the years, but more than that, they had been pioneers of broadcast journalism in a Gulf Coast community in which the new medium of television would be slow to gain a foothold.

Having been in television broadcasting in Colorado since the early 1960s, I had known about Walter Furley for many years. And when my late wife and I moved to Corpus Christi, we often watched his newscasts on KZTV. As a viewer I was hooked by his silky baritone voice, and as a broadcaster I admit to being envious of it. It's the voice most of us dream of, but few possess.

But to me, the most important thing was to learn about the man behind the voice. A man, who had been widely respected, much honored, and deeply loved by his community, a man worthy of biographical examination.

How does one measure the life of a man? His love for his family? His patriotism and love for his country? His love and respect for his fellow man? His ideals, good deeds, and integrity? His faith and love for his church? Walter Furley was all of that and much more.

In general conversation, he spoke with diction so perfect it seemed scripted. He was a kind and caring man, who noticed the little things in life that most of us either take for granted or miss entirely.

For example, in my younger years whenever someone asked me how I was doing, I would answer, "I'm fine; I'm just contemplating my navel." A dumb remark to be sure, but one that always seemed to garner a chuckle out of the recipient.

But the astute, intelligent Mr. Furley was the first person I knew who actually did contemplate his navel. And, with his polished command of the English language, it gave him the opportunity to use the word "omphaloskepsis" in a complete sentence.

The word lies buried in one of my favorite Walter Furley commentaries which begins with the following paragraph: "How does one contemplate one's navel? The navel is the last connection with our mothers in birth of course, and her navel was her connection with her mother and on that generation's to the beginning of time. So it gives one a moment to think about being a continuation of life itself. Right there in the belly button...."

In commentaries such as these, Furley allowed us to see something within ourselves that most of us either miss or take for granted. Those little connections that each of us have to one another.

In another commentary, Furley shared the experience of trapping a troublesome opossum at his home, and when someone from Animal Control came to pick it up, the Furley family was left to wrestle with the millions of fleas the animal left behind. In his commentary, he verbally painted a picture any of us could easily fit ourselves into.

In still another, the patriotic Mr. Furley noted that he was appalled to read that some groups of individuals wanted the United States to adopt a new national anthem. In that commentary he carefully and methodically recited each phrase of the "Star Spangled Banner" word-for-word so beautifully, I remember thinking that in all my life I had never really heard our national anthem before. Nowadays most Americans seem comfortable in accepting the fact that prior to each sporting event, performers use our national anthem to showcase their voices rather than honor our country. And the spectators cheer as the performer adds notes and riffs that don't exist in the original sheet music. It took Walter Furley to point out that perhaps I, as an American, should take a moment and actually listen to the words. In his commentary, Furley noted how perfect it is in the way it honors our great country and its people, closing with these words: "Land of the free and the home of the brave." Said Furley, "We can have no better anthem than that."

Walter Furley was, to say the least, a master communicator. He was a man for whom communication was not just a word or obligation; it was an essential staple in a life full of many challenges, opportunities, and possibilities. He was one-of-a-kind. A stand-out in a world in which most of us, rich, poor or middle-class, go through our daily routines comfortably bathed in mediocrity while in every generation someone standing tall comes along as a champion for all of us—challenging us to lead better lives for our families, our communities, and for ourselves. Such a man was my friend Walter Furley.

Stewart Jacoby
Director of Radio Programming
South Texas Public Broadcasting System, Inc.

Forward

Ann Marie Evans

Looking back at my childhood in the fifties and sixties from the age of sixty-three, my memories crowd together like commuters on a 5:00 train. But there amidst the leather briefcases, the khaki overcoats, the skinny black ties, and the felt fedoras there stands a face, that of Walter Furley, TV announcer at the only station in town.

Television was new to our house and our nation. Although as a child, I had no interest in the nightly news, Walter Furley and his broadcaster partner Gene Looper were stars. Through the 50s and 60s, not only did they report the news and forecast the weather, they announced the schedules, promoted the programming and (except for one guy and his two poodles who peddled refrigerators and air conditioners) starred in all the commercials.

What I will always remember about Walter Furley was his voice, a voice like dark chocolate, rich and deep, comforting and calm.

When I returned to Corpus Christi after college, I got to know Walter as a fellow thespian as a volunteer at the Harbor Playhouse and a companion chorister in the Chancel Choir at First United Methodist Church. It was at the Playhouse that I remember working the crew as sound operator for South Pacific that I got to hear him sing "Some Enchanted Evening" every night for the entire run. Oh, that voice—that marvelous voice.

At church, Walter got all the narrator parts in all the choral pieces of course, earning him the nickname of "The Voice of God." And who better to read with the authority and majesty needed?

Once he retired from broadcasting, that marvelous voice could still be heard through his audio columns on KEDT. I listened intently to each one. I didn't always see things the way he did, but I always enjoyed his voice.

When I was asked to edit this volume, I was honored and humbled. First, I hoped I was up to the task. I can claim that Walter Furley was the only person to catch me in a grammatical mistake in my adult life. But too, Walter was a language purist; I am not. Walter believed we should all speak a proper, standardized English. I prefer a more liquid language, flowing and changing with life. I promise you, in this work I stuck to the rules.

And what a delight this task has been. As I read through each script slowly and carefully, Walter's voice resonated in my mind. Once again I heard that dark chocolate voice. Page after page Walter's voice read his words to me, sang to me, reminded me of his calm, gentle nature.

And so dear reader, I hope you will find the same delight in these pages as I have. I give you Walter Furley, *vox extraordinarium*.

Ann Marie Evans
Editor
Summer 2015

2002

Our Economy

28 September 2002

There is a frustrating opposition in Corpus Christi to anything new to bring in new tourism.

The city council is considering a baseball park near the convention center with a semi-pro team. It almost negotiated a contract with Landry's to develop the T-heads into an even greater tourist attraction. And in each case groups in the city have opposed the ideas, thwarting all efforts to bring more visitors to Corpus Christi.

Since the drop in the oil business, tourism has become one of our most important industries. The Convention and Tourist Bureau reports nearly nine million tourists come to Corpus Christi each year. Nearly nine thousand jobs are created by tourism, and that is five percent of our total work force.

Tourists support our airport, our hotels, our restaurants, and contribute greatly as paying customers at our department stores. It is estimated tourists spend two billion dollars a year in Corpus Christi.

Even if you feel you are not personally affected by these elements, you still benefit. The hotel motel tax alone generates over six million a year in tax revenue. And the sales tax on tourist purchases stays in our city treasury easing the tax burden on local citizens.

And consider the support tourists give to our museums, Harbor Playhouse, the Symphony—the cultural life of our city that needs all the help it can get.

So before fighting the city council at every idea it presents to attract tourists, these opposing groups would do well to support the plans or offer better ones. Saying no too many times can hurt us all.

That's the opinion of Walter W. Furley.

Voting

4 November 2002

Tomorrow's election day, and early voting brought out a high 13% of the voters registered in Nueces county. And that could mean a high turnout tomorrow.

Every election should have a high turnout because the right to vote, *everyone's* right to vote, is a uniquely American right.

Early in our history only white, male property-owners could vote. Ordinary workers could not. Women could not. Anyone outside the white race could not vote. It took years of persuading Congress to grant the right to *everyone* to vote, and that fight often included bloodshed. And even after the right to vote was assured, there were groups who worked to intimidate voters, to keep them from voting, even with threats of death.

Gaining the right to vote has been a hard and bloody fight. No other country in the world has won that right to the extent the United States has.

Yet so few people actually vote. The majority of the people decline to participate leaving a small minority to determine our government and the way we live. This is dangerous. That small voting segment controls the country, and they could conceivably restore those limits on voting. Then once again, many of us would not be allowed to vote.

Voting is one of those rights which, if you don't use it, you may lose it.

Polls are open from seven to seven tomorrow.

That's the opinion of Walter W. Furley.

Armistice Day

27 October 2002 for 11 November 2002

My late father fought in the World War, "The War to End all Wars." He was wounded at Verdun, France, and perhaps with good fortune, for he was evacuated back to hospital just before a fierce battle killed many of his buddies. It was an especially horrible war. Men fought from muddy, rat-infested trenches, and on orders had to climb out, go over the top, and run toward the enemy, while incessant machine gun fire was cutting them down.

Dad was able to come home in 1918, but it wasn't until 1941 he realized he had not fought in "The War to End all Wars," but only the first World War. That war ended with the signing of an armistice at the eleventh hour, of the eleventh day, of the eleventh month, November 11th, which was then designated as Armistice Day, the day to remember the doughboys who died in that war.

Since World War II, we have designated today as Veteran's Day in memory of all those who died for their country in all wars. But Dad always felt November 11th should be special. It was a day of honor for the doughboys.

I couldn't help but recall that "eleventh hour of the eleventh day of the eleventh month" on that September 11th. I was asked to serve on this year's program at Cole Park remembering 9-11. And I remember looking out over the crowd and seeing the groups of people in uniform: The Navy's brilliant whites, the Marines' crisp khakis, the policemen's blue, and the firemen's deep black. It occurred to me that each of those people in uniform could die protecting the rest of us.

And what's more, each of them knew this when they put on that uniform.

They are all our heroes, and all should be remembered not only on Armistice Day, Memorial Day, Veterans Day, and 9-11 Day, but every day. We honor those who have died, but we must not forget, we are living among heroes today.

That's the opinion of Walter W. Furley.

Book Review

17 November 2002

A new book about old Corpus Christi has been published, and I have found it completely absorbing.

It is published by the *Corpus Christi Caller-Times* and is titled *Old Corpus Christi: the Past in Photographs* and the photographs are fascinating, showing how Corpus Christi grew from a tiny fishing village to a big metropolis.

The cover alone is arresting—a causeway to Padre Island was made of wooden planks with ruts to guide the wheels of the cars that dared make the journey. There was a lane for going and a lane for returning but no passing. It was destroyed by hurricanes, but some of the pilings survive today in Laguna Madre.

Many of the pictures have never before been published. Especially interesting are those showing people coming here looking for jobs at the Naval Air Station. There was no housing for them. Most could not afford the few hotels, and they ended up living in make-shift tents on North Beach.

Pictures of Corpus Christi in the late 1800s give faces to names that are still part of our everyday life: Doddridge, Blucher, Belden, Ben Garza, Mary Carroll, Ella Barnes, Menger, Spohn—all people who lived here at the beginning of the last century.

Author Murphy Givens has arranged the pictures in chronological order so you can see how the city grew to be what it has become today. But the feeling that remains after seeing the pictures is Corpus Christi was always a bustling community. Beautiful people worked and lived here, married, had children, built schools, built businesses, and enjoyed leaders who could see what lay ahead for Corpus Christi and prepared for it, for us today.

Old Corpus Christi: the Past in Photographs is a wonderful book, and I hope you get to enjoy it.

That's the opinion of Walter W. Furley.

Priest Scandal

25 November 2002

We all have been disturbed by the scandal afflicting some priests in the Catholic Church. It is not only tragic, but criminal that those we trust can persuade our children to commit horrid acts.

But I am also disturbed by the enormous damage claims made by the victims, often years later. They are awarded damages in the millions of dollars because they were the victims of a crime. But just who is being punished here?

These millions of dollars are not paid by the person committing the crime. They are paid by the church with money we have given and often sacrificed to give as a tithe. Many of us have been victims of other crimes but have not been awarded millions of dollars as a result. Family members have been murdered, and even when the murderer is brought to justice, there are no millions of dollars in damages awarded the survivors.

I feel exposing the criminal priests and punishing them is sufficient justice. Just as punishing the murderer with imprisonment is sufficient justice.

When the church has to pay out the millions, it has to sell property, close schools, and diminish its benevolences to meet the judgment. So it is those who finance the church who are being punished for crimes they didn't commit.

We all regret the pain and suffering these victims have endured, but only the criminal should be held accountable to justice, not the innocent members of his parish.

And that's the opinion of Walter W. Furley.

Buildings

2 December 2002

I was shocked to hear the harbor bridge will have to be replaced because it is nearly fifty years old! I somehow thought it was built to last forever. But then, the old Nueces County Courthouse was built in 1914 and abandoned in 1964, so fifty years seems to be the lifespan of our major architectural efforts.

This summer I went to England, and visited buildings which were nearly a thousand years old. One of the grandest castles, Warwick Castle, was begun in 914 and was being added to up until the last century. And it still stands. Westminster Abbey was built in 1045—still standing. St. Paul's Cathedral in 1673—still standing. All still standing, still being used.

Now one would think builders today would have better construction techniques and materials than builders hundreds of years ago. Yet their structures are standing proudly and are still being used, while we must abandon ours every fifty years.

Next year Corpus Christi plans to celebrate its 150th anniversary. There will be few buildings to commemorate that are more than 50 years old. Why can't we build buildings and bridges that last?

Would maintaining them actually cost more than replacing them? The present Courthouse is already thirty years old, and City Hall about twenty. Like Cinderella's coach, they will likely deconstruct in another ten or fifteen years. So celebrate them while you can. They may be thrown away also like used Kleenex.

That's the opinion of Walter W. Furley.

Mispronounced Words

9 December 2002

I have stood it as long as I can. (super: "nuclear")

The word is NEW-klee-ər, not NEW-que-lər. I know, President Bush says NEW-que-lər. President Eisenhower said NEW-que-lər. Even the past president of the Atomic Energy Commission said NEW-que-lər.

President Carter says "nukier," as though something that is "nuky" can be "nukier." The word is NEW-clear. Say "new" then say "cle-ar"—NEW-klee-ər, and it comes out right every time.

And another word—it is short-LYVED, not short-LIVED.

Anything that is short-LYVED has a short life, not a short live. You can live a short life, but if you do you are short-LYVED.

And another word—"prolly." What in the world is "prolly"? You're "prolly" going to laugh at this, but too many of us say "prolly" for "probably." There's a "bob" in there—PRAH-bob-lee. Don't make it a problem.

It's important we correct these mispronunciations because, as Dr. Bergen Evans of Funk and Wagnalls says, if mispronunciations persist over a long period of time, they tend to become correct.

How ever could we explain in history "prolly," "short-lived" and "new-que-ler." Say them again—PRAH-bob-lee, short-LYVED, NEW-clear.

This is probably a worthless effort, short-lived, and insignificant in the light of the nuclear age.

But one must try to eliminate language pollution.

That's the opinion of Walter W. Furley.

'Twas the Night

9 December 2002

I hope you're all free this Saturday night and can attend the Corpus Christi Symphony Christmas concert. There will be 600 voices singing, the full orchestra playing, and special holiday music from Hanukkah songs to "Rudolph the Red Nosed Reindeer."

I mention the concert because I will be reading "Twas the Night Before Christmas" while the Symphony orchestra plays special music for the poem. It should be very exciting to hear.

The poem, also known as "A Visit from St. Nicholas" was written by a New York city professor who wanted to be known for his academic work. But this poem for his children at Christmas 1822 is the only way the world remembers Clement Clark Moore.

One story says he wrote it while riding in a sleigh to buy a Christmas turkey. But this poem has determined almost all our secular Christmas traditions. His description of St. Nicholas inspired a cartoon by artist Thomas Nast who showed Santa Claus in a fur trimmed suit, about to go down a chimney way too small for him. Moore described St. Nicholas dressed all in fur from his head to his foot but that picture has been altered to show a bright red suit trimmed in white fur.

Moore at first refused to admit writing the poem because he thought it was beneath his position as a famous scholar. Which is odd, because recently a researcher claims that Moore indeed did not write it, but that a gentleman poet of the time, Henry Livingston, Jr., composed the whole thing.

At any rate, it is Clement Moore's name beneath the title, and it is that poem that I will read Saturday night with the Symphony. Concert time is 8:00 in Selena Auditorium. I do hope you are there.

It's going to be an exciting evening.

That's the opinion of Walter W. Furley.

Christmas

December 23, 2002

Several years ago, I was invited to visit an elementary school at Christmas time. I read to the students "The Night Before Christmas" talked with them about the Christmas story, and then took some questions. One little boy asked me very seriously, "Do you believe in Santa Claus?"

He obviously had good reason to wonder, and I suspect Santa Claus had passed him by more than once. I told him, "Yes, I believe in Santa Claus."

And I explained that I thought he was a spirit, that came to visit us all every Christmas, making us want to give something to all we know and love. How else could you explain why everyone has the urge to give Christmas gifts? It's not the television commercials or the colorful advertisements in the newspaper. It's something you really can't explain. You want everyone to have a Christmas gift, and you go to great effort to make sure those you love get something from you on Christmas morning. That's Santa Claus working, I believe.

Even so, I know there are many little boys and little girls who are still asking, "Do you believe in Santa Claus?"

And thank goodness most of us do. Look at the success of the Marine's campaign for "Toys for Tots," the gift baskets prepared by the Salvation Army and many churches, the surprise gifts from one neighbor to another, the extra money to the paper boy.

I know there are still little boys and girls who will receive nothing this Christmas, but believe me, Santa is working hard to reach them. Because I believe Santa Claus is you.

That's the opinion of Walter W. Furley.

Miradores

December 30, 2002

One of the most beautiful additions to the Corpus Christi Bayfront is the line of Miradores, the classic little lookouts lined up along Shoreline Boulevard, facing out over Corpus Christi Bay.

I'm Walter Furley, and it is my opinion that the Miradores have gone under appreciated ever since their first appearance.

The Miradores were built as a memorial to Devary Durrill, daughter of Mr. & Mrs. Dusty Durrill. The young girl was killed in an auto accident, and the suit against Ford Motor Company resulted in the highest damages ever awarded for an auto accident.

Mr. Durrill has used the money to form the Christy Durrill foundation, and it was from this foundation that the Miradores were built and given to the city of Corpus Christi free. They enhance the waterfront as nothing else has since the T-heads were built. They are beautifully built, with Texas granite decorating each one, and a water fountain in each one. Visitors to the city are especially admiring of the Miradores. The entire waterfront has been redefined, and the line of Miradores now a trademark of the city.

So, a long overdue thank you from everyone in Corpus Christi is due Mr. Dusty Durrill for conceiving the idea of the Miradores, then financing their construction, and then graciously giving them to the city.

That's the opinion of Walter W. Furley.

2003

Enron

6 January 2003

Last night CBS presented a drama about the collapse of Enron. According to the story, the fall was caused by the company hiding its debts to make its assets look bigger and thus attract more investors.

What started as a minor deception turned into a fatal corruption. I found the story disturbing.

And I recalled a recent news story that was just as disturbing and may explain how the Enron debacle could happen. A professor at Rutgers University researched the incidence of cheating on campuses since the 1960s, and he found that 87 percent of the students surveyed admitted to cheating. It makes one wonder, how could this be?

It could be because we have all relaxed our habit of following the rules. We run red lights when we think we can get away with it. We fudge on our tax returns when we think no one will notice. Shoplifting of little items like gum or candy is all too common.

Little breaks in the rules strengthen us to make bigger breaks in the rules. Then when we get into a position of great responsibility and power, we find it easy to break even bigger rules. And we end up with disasters like Enron.

There is a good reason to be honest and fair, truthful and loyal. It is the basis of our civilization.

A famous Texas judge, Joe Greenhill, spoke here in Corpus Christi once at a Boy Scout dinner. He said our nation cannot exist without people who want to obey the law. If everyone breaks the law, there cannot be enough police to protect the rest of us. And we will be at the mercy of the lawless.

There was another aspect to that survey of student cheating. Those same students said they saw nothing wrong in cheating. And when teachers faced parents with evidence of their child's cheating, the parents too often refused to believe it and dismissed the charges as something all kids do sometime or other.

Now we know how Enron happened. And how it could happen again.

That's the opinion of Walter W. Furley.

Truan

13 January 2003

I was very moved by the story about Senator Carlos Truan in this morning's *Caller*. He's retiring after 34 years in the Texas Legislature. He is credited with getting CCSU to become part of Texas A&M, helping pass ethics reforms in the House, writing a birth defects registry bill—just to name a few of some major achievements.

The part of the Truan story I find most moving is that about his childhood. His parents divorced when he was a baby; his mother raised the family. So he comes from a single parent family.

We hear this scenario in many court rooms today, and the defense is the criminal comes from a "single parent" family and shouldn't be blamed for wandering aimlessly into a life of crime.

Carlos Truan's mother showed a strength that was to be a model for her son. She went to work as a maid during the week and a cook on the weekends. When Carlos Truan was old enough, he worked to provide the family money by mowing lawns, shining shoes, anything a youngster could do to earn money. He worked hard in school and was president of his high school student body. I suspect he worshiped his mother and would do anything he could to help her and wanted very much to make her proud of him.

I think Carlos Truan has lived the American dream: not just to have a fine house, fine car, lots of money, but to have the freedom to work hard and achieve a fulfilled life.

We're all given talents, but not all of us use them to their full potential. We try to get by doing as little as possible.

Carlos Truan had a talent for getting things done, and he worked hard to use it to survive as a child, to get a good education, and succeed in his business, and then to move into the world of politics, and there achieving not only personal success but making South Texas better for us all.

I know Mrs. Truan is proud of her son, Carlos. She raised him well.

That's the opinion of Walter W. Furley.

Art Center

19 January 2003 (KZTV) and
14 January 2007 (KEDT)

One of the most exciting events this past week was the opening of the renovated Art Center on Shoreline Boulevard. The success of this center is a good example of what can happen when a dedicated group of citizens concentrates on a specific goal.

What is now the Art Center began life in the 1940s during the war. It was the U.S.O. where servicemen and women in the area could relax, enjoy a free meal, but best of all, get to know people in Corpus Christi who volunteered to work there. Many a serviceman found the love of his life at the downtown U.S.O. and when the war was over came back to live here as Corpus Christi citizens.

After the war, the building became a part of City Hall, and when it was no longer needed, was to be demolished, to give the Bayfront a complete open area for a grassy park.

But the art community saw it as a godsend to house the work of local artists. It was a good building perfectly located for maximum traffic. But it took a real fight to persuade City Hall to let them buy it. The artists held fundraisers, solicited donations, worked on grants, and finally opened the first downtown museum for local artists. And its success has demanded more room, a bigger building. And once again that art community worked with gritty determination to get it built and paid for. And the results are spectacular. The Center has not only created a beautiful display place for artists but has greatly encouraged and enlarged the entire arts community. But best of all, it has given Corpus Christi a real show stopper along Shoreline Boulevard.

If City Hall had had its way back in the 1960s, that part of Shoreline would today be only a plot of grass. The lesson to be learned here: don't depend on government or City Hall to build your dream. If you really believe in your dream, do it yourself. That's the way the members of the art city did it. And they did it mighty well.

That's the opinion of Walter W. Furley.

Sundial

27 January 2003

Of all the art set in Corpus Christi public parks, there is one subject that has not been considered and one so obvious for the city.

I'm Walter Furley, and it is my opinion that the perfect art piece for the city of Corpus Christi would be a sundial.

Some of the world's greatest artists have created sundials as major art pieces. They range from the gigantic, to beautiful little spheres that catch the suns rays and leave a shadow on a spot that tells the exact time of day.

Some examples are in the center of park, raised high so the shadow of the gnomon can be seen clearly as it points to the time of day. One is at the Pan American campus in Edinburgh. One is at Disney World in Orlando, Florida and is reputed to be the largest in the world.

Sun dials are perhaps the oldest means of determining the time of day, and of measuring the hours. And they still work. Sculptors or artists would have a heyday imagining a unique and beautiful sundial overlooking the bay.

Since Corpus Christi is a city known for its sunshine, it would seem to me only logical that we should have a monumental sundial on Shoreline Boulevard to emphasize the sunny disposition of the sparkling city by the sea.

That's the opinion of Walter W. Furley.

Sundial

27 January 2003

Along with the improvement of our beautiful Bayfront, I would like to see more public art included.

We as a city are proud of the Ullberg sailfish sculpture, the classic horseman honoring the Falcon family, the first to settle in this area, and the tall steel weather vanes that turn in the direction of the blowing wind.

I would like to add to this list a gigantic sundial. A sundial like those in Europe, and even in some places in America with a gnomon twenty feet tall to cast a shadow on a tiled floor with the hours of the day engraved on it. There could even be a seating area incorporated, so visitors could watch the shadow move across the markings for the hours.

Some sundials in Europe are in the form of human figures whose shadow marks the hours. One at the London Astronomy Science building is in the form of two dolphins, whose tails meet at the top, leaving a hole for the sunlight to shine through and throw a spot of light on the hour figures below.

Surely there are artists in the Coastal Bend who could create a sundial of unique design specifically suited to Corpus Christi. A huge sundial would be a beautiful landmark, a fine meeting place, and an intriguing addition to our Bayfront.

Think about it. It could be a work of art admired all over the world as the "Corpus Christi Sundial" with tourists coming to pose beside it for souvenir pictures. And with our abundant sunshine, there would rarely be a day when we couldn't tell the exact time of day, standard time of course.

That's my opinion. I am Walter Furley.

Pilots

2 February 2003

A year or so ago I covered the winging of new pilots at the Naval Air Station. I was so impressed by them all, but especially so after I learned that only the top students from the nation's schools and colleges were eligible to apply. Then they had to take an entrance exam that eliminated many of them. And each level of flight training found many of them disqualified, so that only the very best were able to make it to the top.

The astronauts we lost this weekend went through even more rigorous demands and training. Many had multiple college degrees. All were superior people working at a very dangerous job. Yet, they each loved their work and experienced and achieved more in their short lifetime than most of us dream about. Though we have lost them, they were able to live the life they loved and live it spectacularly.

A young pilot in World War II, John Gillespie Magee, was killed in action at the age of 19. And some days before his death he wrote these words which every aviator and astronaut could say with him:

> Oh, I have slipped the surly bonds of earth,
> And danced the skies on laughter-silvered wings:
> Sunward I've climbed and joined the trembling mirth
> Of sun-split clouds...and done a hundred things
> You have not dreamed of. Wheeled and soared and swung
> High in the sunlit silence. Hovering there,
> I've chased the shouting wind along and flung
> My eager craft through footless halls of air.
> Up, up the long delirious, burning blue
> I've topped the wind-swept hills with easy grace,
> Where never lark, or ever eagle flew.
> And, while with silent lifting mind I trod
> The high untrespassed sanctity of space,
> Put out my hand and touched the face of God!

Pear Trees

10 February 2003

One of the delights of living in Corpus Christi is to see every winter the flowering of the ornamental pear trees. There seems to be one on every street—large, white snowballs of trees right there amidst the palms and mesquites.

Most of the other trees are bare for the winter. But the precocious pear tree suddenly sprouts thousands if not millions of little white blossoms that completely transform a winter's day.

It occurred to me as I admired the white beauties, that they would look spectacular along our Bayfront. A solid line of them along Shoreline Boulevard, perhaps even out on the T-heads, all flowering at the middle of January and staying in flower through the first two weeks of February. They could be planted alternately with our palms or in clusters along the green stretches of medians. The effect would be much like that of the cherry blossoms in Washington D.C. Tourists would come from miles around to see the white pear trees in spectacular array. We might even start a pear tree festival, like the azalea festivals in many of the southern states each year.

In any event, they would be beautifully white every January and February. Then in the spring and summer, add a new green dimension in contrast to the tall palms already there. If the city could not fund them, perhaps a garden club would care to undertake the project or one generous benefactor. The ornamental pear tree is a beautiful way to end the Corpus Christi winter, and prepare us for the coming spring. And could become another jewel in our beloved Bayfront.

That's the opinion of Walter W. Furley.

CCYAC

17 February 2003

There is a marvelous chance to hear great music this weekend. The Corpus Christi Young Artist Contest is underway this Friday, Saturday, and Sunday at Del Mar College. It has over fifty contestants from nations all over the world entering for prizes of over $20,000. The top winner gets $5,000!

These students are the truly outstanding ones from teachers and schools in Europe, Asia, South America, and Canada as well as the U.S. This contest is considered one of the biggest in the music world.

The piano competitions will be held Friday and Saturday morning in Del Mar's Richardson Auditorium and the string competition in the afternoons at Wolfe Recital Hall. The public is invited to observe from 9:00 a.m. to 6:00 p.m. each day.

The students are eager to come to Corpus Christi for the competition, for they will be judged by world class musicians, so even if they don't win the prizes, they will get invaluable criticism to improve their performance.

But the audience is the real winner. Admission is free, and performances will be truly world-class.

It's like the Olympics in the music world. Only the best will be chosen for the finals, which will be held Sunday afternoon at Richardson Auditorium.

If you have the time, you can spend Friday and Saturday listening to all the contestants, root for your favorite, perhaps even meet and visit with them, and then see whom the judges pick for the final prizes and a contract to perform with the Corpus Christi Symphony.

The Corpus Christi Music Teachers have been sponsoring this contest for 33 years now, and each year, the quality of the contestants has gone higher and higher.

The chance to hear truly astounding young performers in some of the world's greatest classical music is an opportunity afforded a few.

It's free. You'll be astounded at what you'll hear.

That's the opinion of Walter W. Furley.

George Washington

24 February 2003

Saturday was February 22nd, George Washington's birthday. Few people took note of it, because we now celebrate President's Day, the third Monday in February. This was done to lessen the growing number of legal holidays, and to give some of us a three day weekend. I think George Washington deserves his own day and should not be lumped in with all the other presidents.

Washington was unique, not only because he was our first president, but because he lived a life of integrity and honor that should be a model for all presidents, if not all of us. His courage and skill in leading the young Americans to a grueling victory over the oppressive British made him a hero of his time. But he is a hero for our time, too. Washington defined the office of president. He was so beloved at the end of the Revolutionary War, people wanted to make him a king. A lesser man would have accepted, but Washington insisted on the country's leader being a president and only for two terms.

His advice built our government the way it is today, and he strongly influenced the forming of our constitution. His wisdom continues throughout our history, and it is easy to see how our country today would have been quite different had any man other than Washington been its leader. His personal life was honorable, and he insisted on honor among his cabinet.

When he was the commander of the American army, he issued a proclamation banning profanity and cursing among the troops. And you can be sure no one cursed in Washington's presence. He was held in such high regard by his contemporaries, that after his death, a painting in the dome of the capitol showed him being lifted to heaven by thirteen angels, *The Apotheosis of George Washington.*

So, I contend we have had no other president like Washington. His courage and leadership at the birth of our country made him a president among presidents. George Washington deserves a day of honor all his own.

That's the opinion of Walter W. Furley.

Bayfront

3 March 2003

I was puzzled by the action of the City Council last month, when it approved a series of steel awnings and benches along the Bayfront, but very relieved when the Council rescinded that approval.

The steel awnings would have been built if it hadn't been for protests from several citizens, including Dusty Durrill, who is responsible for the beautiful Miradores along the seawall, the comfortable white benches, and the impressive memorial to Selena. And I include the remodeled Art Center on Shoreline Boulevard.

Each of these features conform to a theme, a Spanish Colonial architecture theme that is so appropriate to the city, to the area, and to our history. The Council's plan to put up abstract steel awnings and steel benches in the midst of this old world charm that is enhancing our Bayfront is *really* puzzling.

It is as though the Council has no concept of the Bayfront, and will approve anything anyone wants to construct on it like Ferris wheels and amusement rides.

Dusty Durrill's dream for the Bayfront is one of old world elegance, with a specific theme like the esplanades in Paris, the malls in London, like Central Park in New York. Each has its own ambiance, its own theme that sets each apart as one of the real beauty spots of the world.

That's what our Bayfront is even at this moment. Any additions should comply with the art and design already set, and not become a hodgepodge of some careless construction endeavors.

As for steel awnings, I refer you to the new RTA bus station being built across from Padre-Staples Mall. Imagine this along our Bayfront.

The real concern here is apparently, there is no real plan for the future of our Bayfront. Dusty Durrill's contributions must not become just random constructions there; they should be models for anything to come in the future. And the City Council should devise and plan for just such requirements on any other new ideas for building on the Bayfront. With no plan, with no rules, the Bayfront will end up being a jumble of steel awnings, amusement rides, and tasteless shacks. We need a firm Bayfront development plan. And I think Dusty Durrill should make it.

That's the opinion of Walter W. Furley.

Symphony

10 March 2003

I was interested to read in the Sunday paper that growth in many of the nation's major cities depends on the artistic community there. Large industries are interested in locating in areas were there is a lot of cultural and creative activity to attract the highly-paid executives needed in these industries.

This comes at a time when all the arts are in serious financial difficulty. City and county support of the arts is the first to be cut from budgets in a shortfall. Sunday's article indicated that the arts are as important to a city's progress as are tax breaks and business locations.

The Corpus Christi Symphony is among many over the nation in real danger of not only reducing its season but even closing. Just maintaining the Symphony, managing its season, and keeping good musicians is a very expensive endeavor. The irony is that even if the Symphony season sold out every concert, the expenses would still exceed the income. This in spite of the fact that the musicians play for only a pittance of what they are worth. They play because they love the Symphony. But if they did not have other jobs, they could not afford to perform. And Corpus Christi is so lucky to have the excellent musicians that live here.

So, why should a project that cannot support itself be kept alive? Think on this:

Every Symphony concert brings together fine musicians who have spent many thousands of dollars to learn their art, to say nothing of their lifetimes in practice and performance to perfect it. When they assemble on the concert stage, their minds all concentrated on the music they are making, their energies coming together to create the masterpiece the composer has left us, something transcendent happens—a physical and spiritual connection between us the audience, the musicians on stage, the music written a century ago, a moment of true peace and beauty found in no other place, and something we find all to seldom in our lives today.

We cannot let this art, this Symphony, die. If it does, part of our civilization dies with it. And now, experts say the arts are good for the city's economy. The should therefore be much more generous to the Symphony and all the arts.

The Symphony needs you, and you need the Symphony. Corpus Christi needs the Symphony.

That's the opinion of Walter W. Furley.

Arts Festival

17 March 2003

Last week, I implored the City Council to give more support to the arts community, and this week the City announced an upcoming Arts Festival. The Council obviously had considered the festival before my commentary, but I must applaud their initiative.

The festival will run from the rest of March through April and will feature just about every type of art activity the community has ever experienced. Harbor Playhouse is presenting a hilarious comedy, *Nunsense Two* which has been reviewed and declared a real hit. The two ballet companies in the city are presenting major works, the Corpus Christi Symphony has a special concert for the festival, the Jazz Festival Society will hold a concert, there will be visiting musical artists at Del Mar College and A&M Corpus Christi, the Tejano Academy of Fine Arts will conduct a drum and dance workshop, and there will be an intriguing concert by the Corpus Christi Symphony as it conducts the score to a film masterpiece while the movie is playing. This is more activity than you could find in any other community this time of year. A professor from Carnegie Mellon University recently told the Chamber of Commerce that for a community to grow economically as well as culturally, it must have a strong creative community. The number of groups participating in this arts festival shows Corpus Christi has the creativity.

Now it is up to us to support and attend as many of these events as possible. The festival is also in need of volunteers to help coordinate all the activity. If you would like to help that way, call the Volunteer Center at 887-8282.

Here is a chance to show off the riches of creative arts we have in this city and a chance to make them grow and become even better. Make yourself a promise to go, to attend as many of these arts events as possible. It will delight you, and it will help Corpus Christi.

That's the opinion of Walter W. Furley.

Daylight Saving Time

7 April 2003

Daylight saving time—why do we still have it? It was instituted during World War II to give defense workers more time to work on building airplanes and ships. But we don't need that now in spite of the war on Iraq.

Daylight saving saves nothing. We have to change our lives' schedules twice a year because of an outdated law that Congress has yet to rectify. Why do we put up with this?

We just lie here passively letting an outdated law rule our lives without protesting and demanding Congress rectify the situation.

Rescind the law, and let us get on with our lives normally.

Farmers still have to get up at the same time to milk their cows, daylight saving or no. We still go to work and put in eight hours whether it is daylight or night. That extra hour of daylight at the end of our shift doesn't mean we can sleep any later in the morning.

I was in England this past June and was amazed to see the sun rising at 3:00 a.m. It set around 10:00 p.m. London is that much farther north than Corpus Christi, so they see the sun earlier than we do. But good Englishmen still did not rise until about 6:00 a.m., and stores opened about 9:00 a.m. no matter how much daylight was available.

There are three states that have the courage to refuse to abide by daylight saving—Indiana, Arizona and Hawaii. They have some strange TV schedules, but they seem to not mind.

Why haven't we risen up in rebellion and demanded that daylight saving be abolished? Why do we just sit here and turn our clocks back or forward twice a year with no protest. I would vote for any politician who ran on the platform of abolishing daylight saving time. That one issue alone would improve life for all Americans, and let us get on with important things like sleeping through a sunrise or two.

That's the opinion of Walter W. Furley.

Ethnics

14 April 2003

I was disturbed by an editorial in the Caller this past week lamenting the fact that Hispanics are underrepresented on the City Council, and that low voter turnout was the cause.

I lament the low voter turnout. It indicates a lack of interest in the community government, if not the community itself.

But wanting more of a particular ethnic participation implies one's ethnicity is a qualification for public life. And worse, it implies that ethnic groups vote only for members of their group. I know this isn't so. I've voted for many Hispanics over Anglos in our elections and I'm sure the reverse is true also.

Will we ever be able to stop labeling each other and keeping each label separate and apart from the community as a whole?

What does it matter that we are Anglo, that we are Hispanic, that we are black, that we are Asian? We are all Americans; we all have relatives or friends serving in the armed forces, many in Iraq today fighting for our country. We all have the same goals, to live in peace and prosperity. Continually lumping each of us into separate groups does nothing to unite us and indeed causes resentment and even animosity. We must quit thinking of ourselves as a member of some group, We all are members of one community, one state, one country, one world.

In the words of Rodney King, "Can't we just get along?"

Let's accept the fact that the few voters who voted in our last election chose the best of the candidates available without regard to race, gender, or political party.

So let's support the council and help it make the right decisions for our city. The Council members are scheduling town meetings all over the city on a regular basis. Our attendance at these meetings will keep them informed of our needs and inform us of the progress the Council is making toward those needs.

Lincoln said, "United we stand; divided we fall."

We all need to work to be united, to realize we are all one in this community together.

That's the opinion of Walter W. Furley.

Flowers

21 April 2003

A funeral was held for a member of my family this past week, and we suggested that our friends make memorials instead of sending flowers.

We appreciate the memorials, but we certainly appreciate the flowers sent anyway.

In a practical sense, memorials are better. They support an organization that was meaningful to the family, while flowers, expensive as they may be, fade after a few days.

But those flowers were so comforting to us right at the moment we needed comfort. They meant that our friends felt our loss and sent us real spiritual support. It's true the flowers have now faded, but the comfort lingers on, and we remember with grateful hearts the bouquets and plants sent during our time of grief.

So, I have a new aspect of flowers for funerals. Send flowers. Their beauty brightens a very sad time, and the comfort they bring continues even to this day. Memorials help continue the work and interests of the family, but flowers help so much in the healing.

That's the opinion of Walter W. Furley.

Writing

28 April 2003

Did you see that article in Saturday's paper saying writing is being neglected in our schools? I thought at first it meant handwriting or penmanship, which is actually a lost art.

But no, this report says writing themes, articles, or even lessons is not being taught as it once was, and consequently a fifth of the students in grades 4, 8, and 12 cannot write satisfactory prose. And half of them meet only basic requirements, and only one in five can be called "proficient."

The report also reminds us that writing and composition is how we teach students complex skills of synthesis, analysis, and problem solving—skills which will serve them well throughout life.

The report is by the National Commission on Writing, and it was issued just last Friday. The commission has asked former senator Bob Kerry to head a campaign called "Writing Challenge to the Nation" with a mandate to get writing back into the list of things students must learn. All these tests, TAAS, and TAKS, and SATs, emphasize reading and math, but require little composition writing.

One of the reasons given for not emphasizing writing was teachers say they just don't have time to grade such papers. Have we given teachers so much paper work of their own, they don't have time to teach students how to write papers?

That may be the case. An English teacher with five classes a day with 30 students in a class would have 150 papers to grade overnight, if she assigned a theme. If crowding classrooms with fewer teachers is saving us money, what is it costing in our children's education?

We once characterized a basic education as the three R's: Reading, 'Riting, and 'Rithmetic, which in itself indicates a weakness in spelling, if not alliteration. This report was made by a blue ribbon panel made of teachers themselves, superintendents, and college presidents, people who should know the problem. We should all accept their findings, and unite behind Senator Kerry and his campaign to make sure our students learn to write.

That's the opinion of Walter W. Furley.

Texas Boycott

19 May 2003

I think the Democrats did the right thing to boycott the Texas Legislature this past week. They were protesting an unfair plan to redistrict the whole state of Texas. The plan was devised by Republicans for Republicans. All other parties were excluded. So the Democrats played an ingenious move and left the Republicans unable to conduct any business without them.

However, the current districting plan is hardly fair. How ever did legislators decide it was fair to lump Corpus Christi and Brownsville into one district? The representative from that district has had a hard time sponsoring legislation to help either city without neglecting the other. And I understand the new plan would have split the city of Austin into multiple districts, some reaching out as far as Laredo, just to make sure that the district is largely Republican. That is no way to provide fair representation to the people of Texas. When I was in government class, the practice of stretching district boundaries in and out of certain neighborhoods was called "gerrymandering" and was illegal. Has it now become legal? It is certainly common practice.

Now that the State Legislature is complete again, it should concentrate on creating a fair redistricting, so that the people of a specific area can get the representation to which they are entitled under the constitutions of both the state of Texas and the United States of America.

That's the opinion of Walter W. Furley.

Memorials

26 May 2003

Memorial Day reminds us of the heroes who have given their lives in wars to protect our country. Corpus Christi has erected a number of memorials, and our Walter Furley gives us a tour of them.

Corpus Christi's first memorial to the war dead was a cemetery. In 1845 general Zachary Taylor's army was on its way to fight in the Spanish American War when it bivouacked near what is now Artesian Park. Four members were killed in a boiler explosion, and their burial place became the city's first cemetery, old Bayview Cemetery.

The Civil War dead are remembered by the fountain just under the Bluff at People's Street. It was commissioned by the Daughters of the American Revolution.

The Gold Star Court under the Bluff by Mesquite Street remembers the Nueces County men who died in the first World War. The names of all Nueces County boys lost in that war are on bronze plaques along the Bluff. That war was called "the war to end all wars," and once featured a World War I cannon, but it was sacrificed for scrap metal to help fight World War II.

Memorial Coliseum was built in 1953 and dedicated to the veterans from Nueces County who died in that conflict. Their names are on a large bronze plaque near the Coliseum entrance.

Sherrill Park on Shoreline Boulevard is also dedicated to the World War II dead. And it is the site of memorials to those lost in the Korean War, as well as the Vietnam War.

Another memorial to both the Korean War and the Vietnam War is at the Leopard Street entrance of the County Courthouse. It was erected by the Gold Star Mothers Club, whose members lost sons and daughters in the wars.

These memorials are rarely visited, even on Memorial Day. But they have been erected in great reverence and love by a city that remembers what today's peaceful celebrations cost, and in the hopes that there will never be another war requiring more memorials.

I'm Walter W. Furley.

2006

Pilot's Deaths

20 February 2006

When I was a TV news anchor a few years ago, I covered the winging of new pilots at the Naval Air Station. I was so impressed by them all, but especially so, after learning that only the top students from the nation's schools and colleges were eligible to even apply. Then, they had to take an entrance exam that eliminated many of them. And at each level of flight training, many were disqualified, so that only the very best were able to make it to the top.

The recent loss of one our pilots and his instructor at Naval Air Station Corpus Christi reminds us they are all working at a potentially dangerous job. The two young men we lost knew they were doing dangerous work. Yet, they each loved that work and experienced and achieved more in their short lifetime than most of us can dream about. Though we lost them, they were able to live the lives they loved and live them spectacularly.

A young pilot in World War II, John Gillespie Magee, was killed in action at the age of 19. Just a few days before his death, he wrote these words which every person who flies can say with him:

> Oh, I have slipped the surly bonds of earth,
> And danced the skies on laughter-silvered wings;
> Sunward I've climbed and joined the trembling mirth
> Of sun-split clouds…and done a hundred things
> You have not dreamed of. Wheeled and soared and swung
> High in the sunlit silence. Hovering there,
> I've chased the shouting wind along and flung
> My eager craft through footless halls of air.
> Up, up the long delirious, burning blue
> I've topped the wind-swept hills with easy grace,
> Where never lark, or ever eagle flew.
> And, while with silent lifting mind I trod
> The high untrespassed sanctity of space,
> Put out my hand, and touched the face of God!

I'm Walter Furley.

Grocery Baskets

20 April 2006

This is Walter Furley, and this is the way I see it:

Grocery baskets left in parking spaces should be a crime—a fineable crime.

Trying to find a parking space at the grocery story on a busy afternoon is bad enough. But find one, and then see that there is a shopping cart in the middle of it is maddening. If you want the space, you must leave the car in the middle of the lane, remove the basket, get back in the car, and complete your parking.

What kind of people leave their carts in parking spaces? The stores provide storage spaces in the parking lot, usually just a few steps from any part of the lot, yet the big metal shopping carts are abandoned with no thought of the problems they will cause the next visitor.

I see a real sociopathic problem in this. Abandoning the cart anywhere means the perpetrator is not connected to the rest of society and doesn't care that his actions cause problems. The attitude goes beyond thoughtlessness and carelessness. It shows a complete divorce from the brotherhood of man with no concern for the rest of the world.

I see the same attitude that leaves cigarette butts thrown on the street or sidewalk, empty beer cans littering the roadside, and—and this is a big—used baby diapers left in parking lots.

We are all citizens of our city, our country, really all one family. Each of us should show concern for each other and take responsibility for our actions. Everything we do causes a reaction.

If we leave our area clean and neat, we create a happy impression for the ones following us. Of we leave it littered, we cause someone else to clean up after us, to set things right. Whether it's abandoned grocery baskets, strewn cigarette butts, empty beer cans, discarded used baby diapers—each has a place. And it is up to each of us to keep them in their places to show we like where we live, we appreciate the people we live with, we like a clean safe world. We're not just messing with Texas when we behave so thoughtlessly, we're messing with civilization itself.

I'm Walter Furley, and that's the way I see it.

Mother's Day

20 April 2006

This is Walter Furley, and this is the way I see it.

The month of May brings us Mother's Day, and that means many florists, jewelry stores, restaurants, and other establishments will see a lot of extra spending.

The day to honor our mothers has become very commercialized, as indeed, have many other holidays. But the day is still one of our most beloved, and one which we all enjoy observing, though sometimes the pursuit of an appropriate gift overshadows the real reason for the day.

Mothers should be honored every day of course, be told everyday how much they mean to us, and shown our love in the generous giving of ourselves. That's exactly what they have done for us—given generously.

There are many poems written in tribute to mothers, most of them banal and clichéd, and each one with a deep undercurrent of truth.

I found such a poem recently that I found affecting. Critics will never include it in anthologies of the world's great literaturem but it speaks to us children of mothers. Listen:

My Mother's Garden

My mother kept a garden
A garden of the heart.
She planted all the good things
That gave my life its start.
She turned me to the sunshine
And encouraged me to dream
Fostering and nurturing
The seeds of self-esteem.
And when the winds and rains came
She protected me enough
But not too much. She knew I'd need
To stand up strong and tough.
Her constant good example
Always taught me right from wrong,
Markers for my pathway

That will last a lifetime long.
I am my Mother's garden.
I am her legacy.
And I hope today she feels the love
Reflected back from me.

I am Walter Furley, and that's the way I see it.

Memorial Day

25 April 2006

I'm Walter Furley, and this is the way I see it.

I have the feeling that too often we forget to remember Memorial Day.

Here in Corpus Christi, the veterans organizations always stage a ceremony in Sherrill Park, usually a Naval officer speaks, and the Veterans Band plays march music and "Taps."

But the people attending are, for the most part, the veterans and their families, all of whom have their own memories and do not need a Memorial Day to remember those who were lost.

The rest of us are swimming at the beach, barbecuing in the back yard, or at a city park, and enjoying a day off, a day of freedom given to us by those we forget to remember.

I think every day should be Memorial Day. And every hero and heroine remembered by every dawn's early light. We sing our national anthem, and sometimes give an embarrassed laugh when we can't remember all the words. But they are words well remembered by those who lived it.

Listen.

> Oh, say, can you see, by the dawn's early light,
> What so proudly we hail'd at the twilight's last gleaming?
> Whose broad stripes and bright stars, thro' the perilous fight,
> O'er the ramparts we watch'd, were so gallantly streaming?
> And the rockets' red glare, the bombs bursting in air,
> Gave proof thro' the night that our flag was still there.
> O say, does that star-spangled banner yet wave
> O'er the land of the free and the home of the brave?

Bilingual
10 July 2006

I'm Walter Furley, and this is the way I see it.

Bilingual education is again a subject of heated debate in our schools—whether to use Spanish to teach Latin children how to speak beginning English, or to let them learn it by being immersed in English alone.

I really fail to see the problem. We use English to teach beginning Spanish. And by the end of the course are expected to be immersed in Spanish alone. Also, it is appalling we all aren't bilingual anyway, as close to Mexico as we are.

I've heard that most conversations in all languages are based on only 500 words, and if you know just those basic phrases, you can understand and be understood in any language.

I think the problem is laziness. It's just too much trouble to learn 500 new words or phrases.

But it is not surprising. So many English speaking individuals have never learned proper English. How many times have you heard supposedly educated people say, "Where are you at?"

And will we ever get everyone to learn the difference between *lie* and *lay*? *Lie* means "to recline," *lay* means "to place or put." That's third grade English. But even in song, we say, "I'm gonna lay right down and die!"

And does anyone besides English teachers know what a gerund is? I've even heard educated Englishmen say, "My wife doesn't like me smoking" instead of "My wife doesn't like *my* smoking?"

If the English themselves make mistakes, does it really matter if we do?

Worse, does anybody care?

Dr. Bergen Evans who helped write the Funk and Wagnalls Dictionary said, if words are used incorrectly for a long enough time, then they become acceptable and become correct. No wonder we have trouble sometimes understanding Shakespeare and the Bible. And no wonder we have trouble learning a second language, when we haven't learned our first.

I'm Walter Furley, and that's the way I see it.

Frogs

10 July 2006

I'm Walter Furley, and this is the way I see it.

I have been concerned for the past several years at the dearth of toad frogs—the dark green and brown and black ones the size of your fist. There used to be one or two residing in my back yard, but I haven't seen one in years.

One of my sons loved those toads. A favorite picture of mine shows him grinning happily holding a string which is attached like a leash to a very large toad going for a hop down the street.

But in the past months, I have noticed some very small frogs that are caught in my pool. They cannot jump out of the water because of a concrete lip around the edge, so I must use a skimmer net to rescue them. They are very small, the size of my thumbnail, and very beautiful, a light brown with spots of brown and glittering flecks of gold. I thought they were baby toads and would soon grow into the large toads I miss so much, but I have since learned they are tree frogs, very likely a Rio Grande Chirping Frog or a cricket frog. I have heard the musical chirps at night, but assumed birds made them. I see only one or two of the tiny frogs each morning, and they very well may be the same two who have not learned how to avoid the pool. They are very much worth saving, not only for the beauty, but for the fascinating bit of nature that we seem to be crowding out of our lives.

But the mystery remains: where are the large toads? Did our mosquito spraying also kill all the insects they subsisted upon? Or did the last surviving frog hop too slowly on the pavement and ended up just another road kill?

Perhaps they still thrive in the countryside where no speedsters can crush them on the highways. But their deep croaking sounds are missed in the late evening, when they seemed to tell us all is well. The little chirping sounds I hear now seem to say, "Help us. Help us. We're all that's left."

I'm Walter Furley, and that's the way I see it.

Mosquitoes
26 July 2006

I'm Walter Furley, and this is the way I see it.

Living in South Texas, we know when to expect mosquitoes. We pray for rain, then when we get it, right afterwards come the mosquitoes. Even after dumping all the flower pots and dishes that could collect water for their breeding places, they still come in battalions to attack us and suck our very blood. Even when the city sprays mosquitocide they seem to persist, though reduced in number, and I fear that spraying kills some or our beneficial insects, too, like honey bees or lady bugs. Like the poor, mosquitoes will always be with us.

My wife and I like to walk in the early evening, the perfect time for mosquito attacks. We've tried all the recommended spray repellents including rubbing our arms and clothes with those fabric softener sheets. On a cruise a few years ago, we stopped in Cozumel and bought a tube of repellent called "Cactus Juice" and were assured it was an ancient remedy used by the Aztec Indians. The idea we found appealing, since cactus was everywhere and for the most part useless. It was poetic justice that its juice could be used to help mankind.

Apparently the cactus juice worked, for we did not suffer any bites at that time. But after carefully looking at the label on the Cactus Juice, I learned it was manufactured in Rowlett, Texas and is available in most grocery and drug stores. Still the Aztec story may be genuine, though few Aztecs are known in Rowlett, Texas. But mosquitoes are, and the product seems to work.

While working in my yard the other morning, I noticed a large mosquito feasting on my arm. I had not heard his buzz or felt his bite, but I was fascinated to see him gorge himself on my blood. He took in more than triple his weight, and before I could smash him, he flew off to safety. But there were birds about who could feast in such a fat mosquito, or if he lasted until evening, perhaps a bat would happily consume him.

And I thought my DNA could be flying about with the birds and bats. And what if a cat caught the bird that caught the mosquito that sucked my blood? My DNA could be distributed over a small part of the universe. There was something profound in that thought. But then I realized—the cat fed on the bird, the bird fed on the mosquito, and the mosquito—I wasn't flying about the universe in my DNA; I was nothing but part of the food chain.

I'm Walter Furley, and that's the way I see it.

Mockingbird

22 August 2006

I'm Walter Furley, and this is how I see it.

The mockingbird is the perfect bird to be the state bird of Texas.

It walks about proudly, sings loudly, and acts as if it owns Texas, if not the world. It's an elegant looking bird, soft muted gray with dark tail feathers sporting a white border that is repeated in its wings when it flies.

But it is the mockingbird's song that is so captivating.

One, or maybe two, lives in my neighborhood, and on a late afternoon or early evening it sits atop a light pole or palm tree and sings incessantly. I've tried to imitate its pattern—chim, chim, charee...chirpy, chirpy, chickadee—but it's never the same.

He just sings as loudly as he can, making it up as he goes along. Then at the top of some cadenza, he will leap into the air, do a somersault, and land right back on the pole still singing apparently for the joy of it. I never hear another bird answer, so he must not be calling for a mate.

He is not singing so gaily all the time however. He hates my cat, and in what is likely a defense of his territory, will dive bomb the poor animal though I've not seen any wounds in the feline fur. It may be just a game because the cat will sit still, almost immobile. Then when the mockingbird attacks, will leap up in an attempt to catch him, but he never has, that I have noticed. And then the mockingbird sits nearby on the fence and sings what sounds like a gloating, almost insulting song. The cat stays in its position with narrowed eyes and a slightly flicking tail.

And the mockingbird on the ground is just as self confident. It not merely walks or steps, but like an emperor in his domain, struts about with his tail raised high in the air, his head erect and alert, defying anything or anyone to stop him in his quest.

We Texans like to think of ourselves like that, handsome and beautiful, strong and confident, cocksure of ourselves, putting up with no guff from anyone. If only we could all sing like that mockingbird sings . But that is one trait best left to the mockingbird.

I'm Walter Furley, and that's the way I see it.

Pennies

22 August 2006

I'm Walter Furley, and this is the way I see it.

With everything, and I mean everything becoming too expensive, I now learn that money itself is too expensive to make.

A recent news story said it costs the government one and a third cents to make a one cent penny. Those bright, shiny copper coins that will not buy anything by themselves anymore, cost us more than they are worth.

So, are we going to give up the penny? With our money counted on the decimal system, there must be a place for the penny. If merchants rounded prices up to the nearest nickel or dime, we would protest price gouging. Or if they dropped the price to the nearest nickel or dime, they likely would lose money.

And what would we do with those gas prices—two-seventy-five and ninety-nine hundredths? We'd have to call it two-seventy-six, or drop the ninety-nine hundredths altogether. That may be the best idea anyway.

Those of us who were around in the thirties and forties, remember when you could buy things for just pennies. Some candy was actually a penny apiece. Postage stamps were three cents apiece. Gasoline was actually seventeen cents a gallon. Pennies were worth something then, and we needed them, indeed treasured them.

Today, I see them lying on sidewalks and parking lots, ignored as though they weren't worth picking up. I pick them up, even though my mother said money on the ground was filthy-with-who-knows-what-kind-of-germs.

I strongly suspect the penny will always be with us. Remember when the Treasury introduced the Susan B. Anthony dollar? It was in the shape of an octagon so you could feel its difference from other coins. It was supposed to take the place of the paper dollar bill, which the treasury hoped to phase out. I don't think even coin collectors keep the Susan B. Anthony dollar coin. And we lovingly count out our one dollar bills at the checkout counter. We'll do the same with pennies. My sons like to save pennies in a jar. When it was full, it was a treat for them to go to the bank and let the teller pour them into a counting machine and give them back their value in one dollar bills. But always there were some extra pennies that came back with it to start a new jar.

We may not like change, but we do like to get change back, even if it's a penny.

I'm Walter Furley, and that's the way I see it.

Symphony

12 October 2006

I'm Walter Furley, and this is the way I see it.

The Corpus Christi Symphony opened its season this month to an enthusiastic audience in the Performing Arts Center on the A&M Corpus Christi campus.

Like most concerts it was a psychic experience. All those musicians on stage concentrating on the rhythm of the music, eyes on the conductor leading that concentration, playing the music precisely the way the composer intended, every musician with one thought—to make this music come alive. They are actually breathing the music, their mental energy transforming it into the fascinating sounds we hear. The violins all moving with precision together, bows dancing up and down like a line of ballet dancers. The cellists gripping their instruments like passionate lovers, all tensely leaning forward, moving in tandem as they make the music spill out and fill the hall. The brass section at strict attention, anticipating that crucial entrance, then spiking the air with that brilliant blast that pierces the very walls.

The music becomes more than alive. It becomes an enveloping rapture that surrounds the listeners making them breath in the same rhythm as the musicians breathe, trapping them in the melody that grows and grows, reaching up and up to a heart breaking climax that leaves your breathless.

You know, there is real power in thought, and especially when a group of people is creating the same thought. Psychic energy is stronger than we realize, and when those gifted musicians gather together and concentrate all their thought and energy in to the one goal of making music, it's a force with powers we have yet to understand.

And we as audience become a part of it. The power of the music embraces us. We experience the same physical vibrations, and suddenly we are floating in a psychic world, following the melody to new heights and new delights, as we surrender our thoughts and feelings to the fascination of the musical moment.

Okay. Maybe that's a little florid. But think about this: when enough people think the same way, there could be a war. If there are enough people thinking the same thoughts, there could be peace.

But when you are in a concert setting, and all around you are people breathing in the same music, watching the same musicians giving their all to perform that music, you are united with a force and energy found nowhere else. You come out of the concert refreshed, renewed, rejuvenated, re-created, feeling real joy, feeling you are really alive, and so glad you were there.

Come on out to the next concert. If you stay home, you're really missing something.

I'm Walter Furley, and that's the way I see it.

Halloween

24 October 2006

I'm Walter Furley, and this is the way I see it.

A few days after last year's Halloween, a scrawny black cat appeared in our back yard. My wife likes to leave water bowls and some cat food out each morning for the neighborhood cats and offered some to the black cat. But it seemed terrified of her and hid under the shrubs coming out to eat only after it was alone. This continued for several days, until one day it let my wife pet it on the head as it ate, but immediately afterwards it ran away and hid.

Each morning thereafter, it stayed out a little longer, accepted a pet on the back, until after a week or so it accepted the back yard as a safe place and did not run away, and actually let us pat its head and rub its back. Its fur was rough and coarse, and when it tried to meow, its voice was hoarse, barely sounding like a cat.

We wondered if it had been the victim of some Halloween pranksters, who we've heard like to hang cats by their necks and torture them in some strange rituals. We had heard public service spots on TV warning owners of black cats to protect them on Halloween for this very reason.

But the cat stayed with us, never leaving the back yard as though it was its only place of safety. We named it BC for black cat. And BC became so loving, it was difficult to walk in the yard without its rubbing against our legs, almost tripping us. He felt so secure that if he were in our path as we walked, he just lay there trusting us not to step on him.

Then a few months ago an all white cat appeared under the shrubs. It, too, hid until the food was set out and then would cautiously come out to eat. We wondered if BC would challenge the white cat, but it didn't. Instead, BC would rub up against the white cat, the white cat would rub its pure white head against BC's pure black one, and they were like soul mates. It was as though BC was reassuring the white cat, which is now Snowball, that this was a safe place. They both spend their days lying on the walkway, soaking up the sun, rising only to get a drink of water or a bit of food.

Somewhere, both cats had learned to fear humans. BC had obviously been badly mistreated and has suffered greatly. Snowball was larger and had managed to avoid the dangers that menaced him.

I cannot imagine why a human being would harm any animal, especially as a form of entertainment. I suspect that the people who do that are the people we read about in the newspapers or see on newscasts who have hurt and abused other people.

Halloween is an enjoyable time to make fun of ghosts and goblins and therefore our fears, but it also is a time to celebrate all living things and remind us that while we are living here, life can be a joy, this can be a safe place, if we just show some respect and some love for all living things.

I'm Walter Furley, and that's the way I see it.

Politeness

18 December 2006

I'm Walter Furley, and this is the way I see it.

Were you as appalled as I at the last election campaign? Those who I thought were perfectly respectable people were at each other's throats in vile, aggressive and denigrating attacks in television commercials and newspaper ads.

What ever happened to civil disagreement? What ever happened to respect for your fellow campaigner?

I think it died in our own family life and in our lifetime. We as a society no longer look to Emily Post as the proper and polite way of interacting with each other. Some may say we are more honest in our relations and are quicker to express our disdain or disagreement. But that kind of honesty is not always the best policy. What we say and do can be hurtful and destructive if not done with consideration of others. And the resulting resentment can build up into catastrophic reaction, like physical attacks, like wars.

Learning to say "Please," "May I?" "Thank you," "After you, please," "May I help you?" all may seem trivial, but these phrases reflect a respect for those to whom they are addressed. Anything else reflects a selfish attitude or policy and leaves others feeling deprived or at least ignored. And this frame of mind is the fertile field for growing bullies, criminals, even despots and dictators.

Teaching children to be thoughtful and considerate is nothing more than teaching them to be civil, and the best way to do that is to practice it before their very eyes. If the world could have just one whole generation of thoughtful, caring and polite people, there wouldn't be any more wars, there wouldn't be any ugly political campaigns, there wouldn't be any more crimes against each other.

The idea may seem preposterous and even simple-minded, but it is not new. Someone once said it this way, "Love your neighbor as yourself." Be polite. It just might save the world.

I'm Walter Furley, and that's the way I see it.

Artists

22 December 2006

This is Walter Furley, and this is the way I see it.

Artists may be the most alive people in the world. Here's why I think so:

When you and I look at something, we identify it usually and go on about our business. But artists really look at something. Take a tree.

When an artist paints a tree he must look at every leaf, see how some leaves are bright in the sunlight while those in the shade are darker. The artist can see perhaps a hundred shades of green in that one tree. And he has to see how the trunk stands solidly, how the branches are thick near the trunk then thinning out as they reach upward to the sky. And then paint every detail so that when we look at it, we can say, "That's pretty good painting of a tree."

Or if the artist is painting a rose, he must see each petal, see how the colors change from the outer edges to the center of the rose, how each leaf and thorn becomes part of the grand design.

Or landscapes. The Corpus Christi Bay changes colors every hour of the day, one shade of blue in the morning, almost white at noon as the sunlight is reflected, then going to green in the afternoon.

Really, artists see so much more than most of us do.

And it's true of musicians. While we hear a pretty tune, they hear the mixtures of the notes in chords and hear how they progress with the melody. And they also know how each note is produced on each instrument and the way the volume and rhythm rises and falls within the music.

Wouldn't be wonderful if we all were as attuned to the world as artists are? We would appreciate everything so much more.

Wouldn't it be wonderful if we were all attuned to each other, so we could see the beauty in each face, feel the joy and anguish of every person we know, appreciate the work and effort of all those around us, and be appreciated in return.

We could be, you know, if we trained ourselves the way artists do—study how to paint a picture, study how to play an instrument, study how to know and understand our fellow men. If we could just wake up, be aware, see everything in the world and see the world in everything the way artists do.

I'm Walter Furley, and that's the way I see it.

2007

Choices

3 January 2007

I'm Walter Furley, and this is the way I see it.

We have too many choices in this world. I like to be free to choose in any situation, but when there are so many things to choose, it's confusing.

Take toothpaste. My wife put toothpaste on the grocery list, with the added note, "mint."

But the counters holding toothpaste have all varieties. I was limited to one brand, but that didn't help. Toothpaste with cavity protection, another with whitener, another with built in mouthwash, toothpaste gel, and none indicating the flavor. One tube claimed to have all of the above in one toothpaste. But no visible flavor indicator. I finally chose one that was labeled "regular flavor." Sure enough, it was wrong, but we used it anyway.

Another impossible choice is razor blades. There are two well-known names whose razors I bought, and each did a satisfactory job. But when I went to get a refill, I couldn't remember the style razor I owned, and only the specific type will fit into that razor frame.

And how many blades can one razor hold? A single blade was quite sufficient, I thought, until the double blade came along. Then the triple blade, and I hear there is one now with five blades. Why? I buy only disposable razors now, blade and handle complete.

And in the grocery department look at the rows of different breads. I thought the only choice was white bread or whole wheat. Now, multi grains, specialty grains, French bread, Italian bread, German bread, even English toasting bread. Is there a Chinese bread? Is there an American bread?

And tomatoes! You have to choose between organic tomatoes, hothouse tomatoes, beefsteak tomatoes, Roma tomatoes, cherry tomatoes, grape tomatoes, and a lot of other kinds! What is going on?

Variety is wonderful, but so many choices are just disconcerting. I certainly want variety in my life—to a degree, that is. But so much all at once, please! I feel so much safer in the grocery aisle with generic toothpaste, generic razors, generic foods. But there's no such thing anymore. I wish there were. Then there would be a real choice—fancy or plain.

I'm Walter Furley, and that's the way I see it.

Theater Eating

16 January 2007

This is Walter Furley, and this is how I see it.

I recently read, in the New York Times no less, that the big theaters there are allowing patrons to take drinks and snacks into the theater to be consumed as they watch the play, or musical.

I find this appalling.

We go to the theater or concert to hear a gifted artist perform. His or her performance should command all our attention as we watch and listen in rapt silence. These artists are giving all their very souls can offer in these performances, and to be distracted by the opening of candy wrappers, slurping of drinks, and the spilling of popcorn defeats their purpose of engaging your attention.

Most of us have appeared in amateur theatrical productions. We know how difficult it is to concentrate on the stage, remember lines, work up emotions and character interactions to carry the play and tell the story. A good performance involves the audience as each member relates to the actors on stage and waits expectantly to hear what will happen. With people eating and drinking out front, not only are the actors distracted but also the rest of the audience.

You know, ticket prices in New York now average $100 each. For that price we audiences expect a top flight performance, something that completely absorbs us and makes us forget where we are, takes us out of ourselves and into a different world with new characters and new stories. To have to endure people next to you concentrating on eating would be a waste of the $100 you paid for your ticket.

I think before you go to a theater performance, you should ask if eating or drinking is allowed in the auditorium. If so, don't buy a ticket. I don't care whether it's *Lion King* or Metropolitan Opera. You can't possibly enjoy a great performance in such an atmosphere.

Those who insist on popcorn and sodas as they watch a show should limit their attendance to football games or television. The performance on stage should be the only source of nourishment they need.

I'm Walter Furley, and that's the way I see it.

Gatlin

2 February 2007

I'm Walter Furley, and this is the way I see it.

At the opening concert of the Corpus Christi Symphony, the guest artists were the Gatlin Brothers. Their country western style music was well done and enthusiastically received, and incidentally, raised some much needed funds for the Symphony.

At one point, Larry Gatlin complimented the orchestra members for their expertise in performing, admitting that he did not read music and could play only one instrument, the guitar. He noted the years of education it took for these orchestral musicians to learn their craft and the talent they showed in performing. Then he said something to the effect that he may not be as accomplished a musician as each of them, but he bet he had a bigger house than any of them.

The observation brought a big laugh, somewhat rueful, but it pointed out that performing popular music was better paying that playing in a symphony orchestra.

Larry Gatlin also pointed out how he and his brothers spent years trying to break into the country music scene in Nashville, often living on peanut butter sandwiches, and in perpetual suspense as to whether they would make enough in the clubs to pay the rent. Their breakthrough recording of their song "All That Gold in California" put them in the top list of performers, and they've been successful ever since.

Which makes us wonder: why don't all musicians strive for that hit record? Why do they remain content to perfect their expertise on a violin, or piano, or other classical instrument, perhaps teaching for an average salary, and playing in the Symphony for a pittance for pay?

We all must make such a choice. Do we want to spend years living hand to mouth, sacrificing comfort, and even delay starting a family, trying to make the big time? Or do we want to enjoy a comfortable life and what talents we have just for the pleasure they give us?

We certainly admire the performers like the Gatlin Brothers, but we realize the price they paid to get where they are. But then everything costs something. Fame costs intense concentration and practice. It costs broken relationships. It costs loss of what we would call a "normal" life. There's a line in the musical *Fantastiks* that says, "Please God, don't let me be normal."

We who chose the "normal" comfortable life pay for it by giving up the chance to break into the big time to be admired on stages and screens all over the world. But the famous and the normal have one thing in common—we each choose the way we live, doing what we love.

Larry Gatlin's joke about his being less accomplished than the Symphony members, but having a bigger house than they was amusing.

But I wish he hadn't said it.

I'm Walter Furley, and that's the way I see it.

College Concerts

26 February 2007

I'm Walter Furley, and this is how I see it.

We music lovers are missing out on a lot of free concerts.

The music departments of Del Mar and Texas A&M Corpus Christi and Texas A&M Kingsville are presenting regular concerts throughout the year featuring not only students but faculty performers. The ones I have attended have been top notch both in music selection and performance. Each college has a fine group of teachers who are expert on their particular instrument and present truly professional performances equal to what you would pay many dollars for in larger cities.

The student concerts are also very satisfying and often amazing with burgeoning talents from such young and eager pupils. Most concerts are about an hour long and are presented at easily accessible times, and as I said, are free.

Also a great pleasure are the concerts by the choruses in the city. Both Del Mar and A&M have fine vocal groups, and while there is usually a charge for their concerts, the prices is minimal and barely covers the expense the groups incur in acquiring music, and in some cases, paying for rehearsal space.

These concerts are presented by aspiring artists who love to perform for the public after spending untold hours practicing and rehearsing. Their offerings enrich our community and deserve our support. And that support gives you an added supply of great pleasure. It is very likely you will be hearing students perform today who will someday perform with national orchestras or even become world class soloists. While they play for their own pleasure and perfection of their art, they are often disappointed at the small number of people who turn out to hear them.

It takes some effort on our part to find out the dates and times of the concerts, but a phone call to the music departments will avail you of any information and get you on a school mailing list. Attending these concerts is a real form of symbiosis. The concerts provide us great pleasure in listening, and we provide them great pleasure in applauding their efforts.

I'm Walter Furley, and that's the way I see it.

Drug Addict

26 February 2007

I'm Walter Furley, and this is the way I see it.

I think drug addicts are not only self destructive, they are also traitors to their country. Here in our democracy called America, we each have the obligation to make our country the best it can be. And the way to do that is to *be* the best we can be, that Army recruiting slogan notwithstanding.

To deteriorate your body and your mind by recreational drugs cheats yourself not only of your great potential to do and learn wonderful things, it cheats your country of the creative energy and potential power you could give it. You could be the next Thomas Edison or even Abraham Lincoln if your mind and body were free of drugs.

And here's something worse. Those drugs cost you big money, money you usually don't have. You are forced to get it by stealing it, breaking into peaceful people's homes to rob them, even resorting to harm others to get their money to support your drug habit.

And the money you spend on drugs goes to the billionaire drug lords, the biggest of whom are in terrorist countries where drugs are grown as a cash crop. And the drug lords are financing the terrorists who are killing our service people now trying to bring peace to an already ravaged part of the world.

Think about that. The money you spend on drugs is buying the guns and ammunition that kill our brave Americans fighting abroad. Each sniff of cocaine you take, or each injection of heroin you make is causing the death of some heroic American fighting to give you the right to live this drug-driven life you've chosen. Courageous Americans fighting and dying to give you a life of freedom that so many in the world do not have. And what are you doing about that? With each sniff, each injection, you can kill a brave American fighting for you overseas.

Can you live with yourself knowing that?

If you are using drugs, even buying drugs, you are betraying your country. You are a traitor and do not deserve the blessings and freedoms for which so many others are sacrificing, even their very lives.

Stop using drugs. Stop killing your fellow Americans.

I'm Walter Furley, and that's the way I see it.

Marble Falls

22 April 2007

I am Walter Furley, and this is the way I see it.

Recently I returned to the Central Texas town where I was born and visited the plot of land were our homestead had been. All that was left was a vacant lot and a lonely elm tree.

Gone was the two bedroom frame house with the wrap around sleeping porch, the Victorian gingerbread trim, the tall chimney that guarded the fireplace in the living room where native cedar trees were decorated each Christmas. There had been two huge trees in the yards, a chinaberry tree in the front yard and a mesquite in back from which hung a very long rope swing. Both trees had been exciting playgrounds for four growing children, as well as their neighbors and cousins. But the trees are gone now.

The two large vegetable gardens are covered over with paving, and there was no trace of the barn and cow lot where we milked two friendly Jersey cows twice a day and played in the hay stored in the loft. Part of the barn was caged for a flock of bantam chickens, which we children called Bantys and treated them like pets. Their eggs were too small to eat, so we always let the mother hens hatch them to our great delight, as the tiny chicks emerged to take charge of the entire barnyard.

I wondered when the warm, loving house had been destroyed. It was very old then in the thirties, and its lumber could not have been of any use. I hope they, whoever they are, didn't burn it. Marble Falls is famous for a gigantic granite mountain just outside the city limits. And a piece of granite from that mountain was our front door step. It was over a foot thick and measured at least three by five feet. What could have happened to it? Its massive weight would have required some heavy lifting by someone.

Most of the house lot was paved over, the very place where we worked a wonderful garden—turnip greens, English peas, black-eyed peas, okra, tomatoes, potatoes, Kentucky Wonder green beans—each plant inspected daily by us children to remove the big green worms that liked the garden, too. And because Mother loved big red poppies, there was a row of them by the fence. They had a very disagreeable smell, however, and were best enjoyed by just being looked at.

All that's left on the lot is that elm tree, the one remaining thing which might have remembered me, but it had been cut back and trimmed so much it could no longer provide the shade in which we children played.

Nothing stays the same forever, does it? That elm tree has aged just as I have, and likely was aging long before I knew it. Even the everlasting hill that was Granite Mountain had a massive gash in it where the glossy pink stone had been blasted way, and moved to far away places, much of it here to Corpus Christi to form the seawall and the jetties at Port Aransas and Port Mansfield.

Hundreds of years ago, Indians roamed that very spot were I grew as a child. I wonder if they could come back, what they would see and remember. Indeed, hundreds of years from now, who will look on that same spot and wonder: did someone ever live here, and were they happy? I could tell them, "Yes we were."

I'm Walter Furley, and that's the way I see it.

Virginia Massacre
22 April 2007

I'm Walter Furley, and this is how I see it.

I was just as appalled, aghast, and overwhelmed as you were by the mass murders in Virginia this past week. The young man who shot his classmates, his teacher, and himself prepared a video and wrote letters that showed how hurt and angry he was at those whom he thought had mistreated him. Those video and letters were a scream for help and deep cry for attention, for approval, for love.

He accused almost everyone of ignoring him, dismissing him, insulting him, when most barely knew him because he kept himself so withdrawn and unresponsive. He felt mortally wounded because no one seemed to like him. It is this same attitude found in every case of such killings. Many of the murderers claimed to have been bullied and insulted by classmates to the point of not being able to stand it anymore. They couldn't stand feeling nobody liked them or nobody loved them.

It occurs to me that many of us have been curt with acquaintances who annoy us in someway or perhaps to whom we show a general dislike. Could such treatment have triggered a response like that on the Virginia campus? A remark or attitude, that we thought meant nothing at the time, grew into a resentment, then a hurt, then a vengeful rage that exploded in a murderous attack even years later?

What if such a shy, insecure person were given a gentle compliment in a time of great self doubt, was able to build on that compliment until he felt some sense of self worth instead of a desire to pay back those who dismissed him as something of no consequence.

We all tend to respond in a fit of pique or even anger at someone who annoys us, creating a fertile field for resentment and a desire to "get even" in someway.

Look back at your own life. It was the time someone told you what a good person you were, what good work you did, what potential you had that made you feel productive and helped you build a positive self image.

It was someone, somewhere who started that young man in Virginia to feel unwanted, unliked, and even unloved, some word spoken years ago that started a resentment that smoldered and burst into a blazing murderous fire last week.

Words can be weapons that kill or balms that heal.

If we all could thoughtfully and respectfully respond to those who irritate us or cross our way, instead of insulting them, even be polite to those who might offend us, there just might be no terrible attacks such as that in Virginia, or Columbine, or any of the other school shootings that have appalled us over the years.

Maybe your mother was right: always be polite and respectful. It just might save your life.

I'm Walter Furley, and that's the way I see it.

Dollar Coin

14 May 2007

I'm Walter Furley, and this is how I see it.

I received one of the one-dollar coins the other day, and marveled at its handsomeness, the fine intaglio of George Washington and the clever way the inscriptions of "In God We Trust" and *"E Pluribus Unum"* were on the outer edges of the coin instead of on the face and of course the gold color. Not real gold but gold color. Then I put it in my pocket along with all the other coins, and forgot about it. When I needed a dollar later, I went for my wallet and used a dollar bill forgetting about the gold dollar in my pocket.

And wouldn't you know it? Later I used that dollar coin with a dime to buy a thirty-five cent item. I thought it was a quarter. So did the cashier, who wasn't any more familiar with the gold dollar than I. It was about the same size as a quarter, so why should I have to really look at it to see if was a quarter or a gold dollar?

It was then I realized that we use coins according to their size. A penny is one size, a nickel another, a dime, a quarter, a fifty cent piece—they all look like what they are. You don't have to pick them up and read them to see what denomination they are.

That's why all those attempts by the U. S. government to make us use dollar coins have failed. The last one I remember really using as a dollar was the Eisenhower dollar, but I still relied on the dollar bills for the most part. Then came the Susan B. Anthony dollar which I don't remember using at all, and the Sacagawea dollar which was especially beautiful, but did not look like a real dollar. And that's the problem right there. These new dollars do not look like a dollar. A dollar ought to look like a silver dollar, larger than all the other coins and easy to spot.

But then, who wants to carry a pocket full of big coins when you can put several paper ones in your wallet and never notice them until you spend them. The dollar coin may be a lost cause, but if the US mint is going to persist in making dollar coins, at least make them look like a dollar.

I'm Walter Furley, and that's the way I see it.

Harbor Playhouse

14 May 2007

I'm Walter Furley, and this is the way I see it.

We have a very good theater group here in Corpus Christi called Harbor Playhouse.

We know some children involved in the current production called "Honk." I thought it was a children's show, but it turned out to be a very clever satire, which was a big hit in London before coming to this country, and had some very mature ideas to express about family life, love, and prejudice. It is based on Hans Christian Anderson's "The Ugly Duckling." Funny, witty, and very well produced with inventive costumes and scenery, some very clever songs, but most of all some very good performances. Several are good enough to be called professional. But the really satisfying thing was the way each of the performers really threw themselves into their part with great energy and enthusiasm. That of course indicated some very good directing.

It is very easy to see some of those young performers going on to big things in theater the way Corpus Christi's Lou Diamond Phillips did, or Barbara Barrie, or Farah Fawcett, or Selena, or Freddy Fender.

I think perhaps we should work on our attitude toward community theater. Instead of going to any local theatrical performance and expecting a Broadway quality show, we should go just to support the efforts of our local talent. And there is a great deal of truly good talent in our community. In every show there is some actor or singer who is surprisingly good, leaving you really amazed at their talent and wanting to see them perform again. That is certainly true in the current production of "Honk." It's a musical with piano and drums, and it's a comedy. What's more it's enchanting not only for children but us grownups as well. It is playing weekends through May 27.

When Broadway shows do come to Corpus Christi, tickets are from $50 to $75, and sometimes you are disappointed. But at Harbor Playhouse, for $12 you will come away pleasantly amused, and thoroughly satisfied, and perhaps a little surprised.

I'm Walter Furley, and that's the way I see it.

Hummingbird

14 May 2007

I'm Walter Furley, and this is how I see it.

Humming birds just make you feel good.

I've been watching my red hummingbird feeder the past few mornings and seen no humming birds at all, which means I suppose, they have all migrated back north to their breeding ground and where more natural nectar is available to them.

But each fall and each spring, I mix my one part sugar to four parts water, put it in the several feeders I have, hang them in my patio, and wait for their arrival. They are such small, fragile creatures. They excite you with wonder of how they could be, how do they survive in a world filled with hawks and cats and owls that feed on birds.

I suppose their unbelievable speed is what saves them, but they are definitely survivors. And thank goodness they are.

Looking at them through binoculars you see the iridescent sheen of their feathers, sparks of green and blue and black, and if you are lucky enough to attract a male, that bright red throat. They are living marvels.

And I shudder to think that the ancient Aztecs and Incas would kill them and use their feathers to make headdresses and even cloaks. And while you marvel at the natives skills at working with those microscopic feathers, you have to be somewhat horrified to think of how many little birds were killed to make a cloak for a very vain king or queen.

But it is the living humming bird that remains ever fascinating. Their little wings beating so fast you can hardly see them. They look like two ghosts hovering beside the bird, holding it up to drink from the flowers or my feeder. How do they hold still enough to drink, then dart away so quickly when they are through? It is incomprehensible how they are able to take enough nectar or sugar water to create the energy it takes to move those wings so fast they become a blur. And then you must consider that in the fall migration, they fly all the way across the Gulf of Mexico to their summer home, then repeat it again in the spring as they fly north.

Humming birds can fill you with wonder at how they look and how they live. Their presence seems to validate me. My garden was good enough for them to visit, and my sugar water was just what they wanted. But as I said, just seeing them makes you feel good.

I'm Walter Furley and that's the way I see it.

Saving Soap

25 May 2007

I'm Walter Furley, and this is the way I see it.

I have a tendency to "save" things, like used paper clips, extra screws and nails, half used pencils, et cetera, all of which have a potential use, but which also take up an enormous amount of room as clutter. I attribute this to the fact that I was a child of the Depression because my father did the same thing. But there may be a deeper meaning to the tendency.

When my bar of bath soap is reduced to a sliver, I always try to adhere it to a new bar so that it is used right down to the last drop—a sort of continuum that keeps that bar of soap alive and working to the very end. My mother once had a jar of fruit with that same philosophy. I forget what she called it, but the preserved fruit was kept in a large jar with a cloth covering, and allowed to ferment. Every so often, Mom would add some fruit of some kind, peaches, canned cherries, pears, even pineapple, the new fruit mixing with the old to keep the recipe fresh and live. It was delicious on a slice of pound cake or ice cream. But she claimed the original mixture was over a hundred years old, that Aunt Nellie had kept such a jar going for all her life, and if anyone else wanted to start one, she would give them a generous sample, and that fruit compote kept on giving year after year to more and more people. I have a friend who keeps a starter going for sour dough bread, and to keep it alive, makes bread quite often, saving the yeasty starter for the next batch. It is so intriguing to think that I am eating a bread roll, or a fruit compote, made from a starter that was first created years and years ago.

The whole process is something like a microcosm of all creation. Seeds we plant are from plants that have been here thousands, if not millions of years. Every form of life has within it the sperm or egg to reproduce itself and stay alive forever, we hope.

Even we humans are each the product of the thousands of generations who begot generation after generation, so that we are the result of our ancestors passing on their genes to keep the human race going. We're all a part of something vastly eternal. And a part of a future that is infinite, a sliver of life, the result of all that's gone before, and a part of all that is to come.

And so it is that I am keeping the past alive for the future when I take my sliver of soap and stick it to the side of a new bar of soap just to keep things going.

I'm Walter Furley, and that's the way I see it.

Memorial Day

28 May 2007

I'm Walter Furley, and this is how I see it.

Memorial Day is past, but how did you observe it this year? A day off, fun things to do?

The sacrifices of our war dead are worth remembering every day, not just one day of the year. The families of those lost remember, and they don't need a special day for it.

Memorial day is one of our biggest holidays in terms of a day off and fun things to do. Corpus Christi has erected a number of memorials to help us remember, but you may have never seen them because they are rarely visited.

The city's first memorial to the war dead is a cemetery. In 1845 General Zachary Taylor's army was on its way to fight in the Spanish American War when it bivouacked near what is now Artesian Park. Four members were killed in a boiler explosion and their burial place became the city's first cemetery, old Bayview Cemetery, located at the end of Carancahua by Highway 37 in the Hillcrest area.

The Civil War dead are remembered by the fountain just under the Bluff at Peoples Street. It was commissioned by the Daughters of the American Revolution.

The Gold Star Court under the Bluff by Mesquite Street remembers the Nueces County men who died in the First World War. The names of all Nueces County boys lost in that war are on individual bronze plaques along the Bluff. That war was called "The War to End all Wars," and once featured a World War I cannon, but it was sacrificed for scrap metal to help fight World War II.

Memorial Coliseum was built in 1953 and dedicated to the veterans from Nueces County who died in that conflict. Their names are on a large bronze plaque near the Coliseum entrance.

Sherrill Park on Shoreline Boulevard is also dedicated to those World War II dead. And it is the site of memorials to those lost in the Korean War, as well as the Vietnam War.

Another memorial to both the Korean War and the Vietnam War is at the Leopard Street entrance to the County Courthouse. It was erected by the Gold Star Mothers Club, whose members lost sons and daughters in those wars.

And now there will inevitably be a memorial to those lost in Iraq.

And it will become among those memorials rarely visited, even on Memorial Day. But the memorials have been erected in great reverence and love by a city that remembers what today's peaceful celebrations cost, and in the hopes that there will never be another war, requiring more memorials. Perhaps we could visit these memorials more often than once a year and remember what they cost.

I'm Walter Furley, and that's the way I see it.

Plastic Bags

26 June 2007

I am Walter Furley, and this is the way I see it.

Several years ago my family spent a summer in Guadalajara, Mexico. A beautiful city with lots of flowers, good food, and many things to see. But in our daily life we were surprised to find that on our visits to Mesa Rica, the local grocery store, they offered no free plastic bags in which to carry our groceries. Customers brought their own grocery bags, usually woven tote bags, very durable and used on every visit to the grocery store. The store conveniently sold such bags to the likes of us who didn't bring our own, so we quickly adapted to the custom.

Now here at home we are offered the choice of "paper or plastic," and it's so easy to take the plastic bags because they're easier to carry when full. The paper bags often need two hands—one to hold the sack, the other to support the bottom. But these plastic bags have become positively ubiquitous. They're everywhere: on trees, on power lines, blowing in the streets, floating on the bay waters where they are fatal attraction to sea life.

Well, when a new grocery story opened recently, we noticed they were selling nice canvas bags for carrying groceries home, just as we did in Mexico. So on a whim we bought a couple of the bags and now use them on every trip to the grocers. No more plastic bags choking up our pantry, littering our yard or street. And as a result, we feel we're doing something to save the environment. Plastic bags never die, you know; they will be here thousands of years from now for anthropologists to ponder over.

So I can highly recommend using your own tote bags for trips to the grocers.

No matter how you store those plastic bags, they multiply exponentially ending up stuffing your closets, taking up space needed for other things. Also using your own tote bags, you don't have to remember to take them back to the store for recycling.

Listen, every bit of time and effort you can save is a good for you and good for the country.

I'm Walter Furley, and that's the way I see it.

Sandals

26 June 2007

I'm Walter Furley, and this is the way I see it.

When I was on military duty in Japan, I and most other Americans there were struck by the simple footwear the Japanese used.

Just a shoe sole, it seemed, with two strings that came between the toes and back to the sides to hold it on. A very efficient and inexpensive sandal. The Japanese wore them exclusively, it seemed, everywhere and with good reason. They could walk through water puddles and suffer no damage; they could slip in and out of them easily, which was very important since the Japanese do not wear their shoes in their houses.

So it was no surprise to see many of the Americans making similar sandals out of old tires with the double strap attached. That would seem to be the end to it, we soldiers using a Japanese style for our own comfort. That was in 1951.

And you know what happened. The GIs came home with their sandals, and everyone wanted them. They were great at the beach, great for all casual wear, and just plain comfortable, and cost next to nothing.

So naturally American manufacturers, being the opportunists they are, began making their own versions and selling them for a nice profit. We named them "flip flops."

Now those cheap and easy flip-flops have become high style. Men's versions in fine leather cost as much as regular shoes. And the versions for women—wow! I was in an exclusive store in Austin recently, and noticed on sale were jeweled flip flips for nearly two hundred dollars. There is even jewelry with flip-flop designs, cute little sandals of gold and rhinestones to wear on a necklace. And I must admit those flip flops do look attractive on a lady's barefoot with painted toenails.

There's a lesson here, if not a moral.

No matter how simple or lowly we might regard anything, it can always grow to become something quite valuable and coveted. They say during the French Revolution the poor people had no food and were reduced to eating snails. Now, go to a fancy French restaurant—escargot, anyone?

I'm Walter Furley and that's the; way I see it.

Oklahoma

7 July 2007

I'm Walter Furley, and this is the way I see it.

A big surprise awaits you at Harbor Playhouse this month.

A new production of the Rodgers-Hammerstein musical *Oklahoma* opened last week to an audience that couldn't applaud loud enough.

It was pleasant to hear all the old melodies and songs and hear the great comedy lines we've all but memorized, but Friday night's production at Harbor Playhouse was so refreshing, so energized, and so beautiful, it was just great fun.

The show has fine voices and a terrific chorus. And there was a real orchestra and a pretty good one, too. But the thing that really got the audience was the spectacular dancing. Every character who was scripted to dance, danced delightfully well, and the ensemble dancing just evoked roars of approval. The real knockout, however, was the dream ballet. Beautifully staged, marvelously lit, and truly exciting dancing. This was much more than any amateur production could expect.

The major credit for the production has to go to its director Joel Earley. His concept of the show, his giving each principal a star turn on stage, and his keeping the show moving so fast, you forgot you knew the show but kept wondering what's going to happen next. He would no doubt give credit to his actors, each of whom delivered, spot on.

But it was the chorus that made the show, that made you stand up and cheer. When you go, get prepared for a spectacular surprise finale. It left the whole theater ringing and the audience singing.

The Harbor Playhouse can be proud of its production of *Oklahoma* and you will be, too. It's playing weekends through this month.

I'm Walter Furley, and that's the way I see it.

Public Clothing

7 July 2007

I'm Walter Furley and this is how I see it.

I know I'm older than most of you listeners, so that makes me old-fashioned, but old-fashioned or not, I am appalled at what some folks wear out in public nowadays.

Yes, nowadays. That's the way we old folks talk, you know.

But when I see people going out in public wearing what was once called underwear, I can't help but think, don't they know people are looking at them? Boys and men wear oversize T-shirts over a pair of flimsy shorts, with flip flops on their feet, and a baseball cap worn backwards. That's what you should wear if you are mowing the yard or working where no one will see you.

And the girls and ladies aren't much better attired. Many are content to wear the same costume, T-shirt, shorts, and flip flops. But the ladies go even further in a lack of discretion: halter tops which are barely brassieres, shorts that are briefer than lingerie, and high-heeled sandals. I'm sure it's all very comfortable to them, but seeing it makes me feel embarrassed, and I try to look away, not always successfully.

And another thing:

I can understand wearing jeans (for some reason I tend to call them dungarees) with occasional holes or patches. But buying them brand new with knee holes and raveled edges and paying nearly $100 is beyond my comprehension. And to top it off, this attire is now even seen in church services. But that's a whole other subject.

Most of us old folks grew up thinking when you go out in public, you ought look at least decent, if not your best. Certainly, looking nice was something to strive for.

It's a new world, now, and my world is one these youngsters will never know, and perhaps never want to know.

But (and I'm saying "but" a lot today) but what you wear and how you act is all a matter of respect. It's how you show respect for the people around you and how you show respect for yourself.

So, out of respect for the young people's fashions of the day and respect for their own taste, I'll say no more about it. But...

I'm Walter Furley and that's the way I see it.

Summer Drinks

19 July 2007

I'm Walter Furley, and this is how I see it.

These hot summer days remind me of similar seasons in my youth here in Corpus Christi with an advantage I fear young people today do not have.

It was a favorite root beer stand. I seem to remember it on Morgan Avenue with a small building on the back of the lot and a row of parking spaces in front covered by corrugated tin roofs. We teenagers after a church meeting or just on a whim of getting together would pile into a car forcing it to hold as many of us as physically possible and drive to the root beer stand. Few cars were air conditioned then, so the hot evening and crowded automobile required immediate relief. And that relief came in the form of "Black Cows," big scoops of vanilla ice cream in an icy mug filled with the root beer. So cold and so delicious, and if I remember, so inexpensive—only 25 cents a mug.

And you could get variations. "Red Cow" was cherry soda over ice cream; "Purple Cow" used grape juice.

A car stuffed with sweaty teenagers, singing, laughing, and joking was immediately quieted and cooled down when the girl car hop would bring out the tray loaded with icy mugs and drinks. That ice cream and soda was so satisfying and cooling, it was the perfect ending to summer day. And something to look forward to eagerly the next time.

I know of no such drink stand today. With a whim of nostalgia, I bought a carton of ice cream and a bottle of the root beer just to try out the old recipe. It was still delicious, but in my air conditioned den I was conscious of the high calories and limited the serving to an iced tea glass.

The memory was incomplete without my old school mates and friends. And in trying to remember them all, I realized how few are still around and wondered what happened to them after those fun filled summers, and what happened to the root beer stand.

It's all just not here anymore, like so many things in life.

I'm sure youngsters today have their own memories to cherish, but I wonder if they are as sweet as those we shared when we all filled up that old Ford sedan and went searching for Black Cows.

I'm Walter Furley, and that's the way I see it.

College Costs
20 July 2007

I'm Walter Furley, and this is how I see it.

I was talking to a young high school graduate recently, who had been accepted by an Ivy League college on scholarship. But he wasn't going to the eastern college. He said the scholarship was for "only" ten thousand dollars, and a year's tuition was fifty thousand.

That's just one year. Four years would be two hundred thousand dollars. Luckily, a public college gave him a scholarship that covered almost all tuition, so he has to be content knowing that at least he was good enough for a partial scholarship at the big eastern college.

A recent story on CNN set the average cost for a year at a public college at just under three thousand dollars. That plus room and board adds up to almost thirteen thousand a year. Full time students at private schools pay an average of thirteen thousand dollars a year which added to room and board comes to over twenty-two thousand dollars a year.

And most students get student loans to pay for their education and upon graduation have a huge debt to face before they even get a job. Something is just not right here.

Most parents I know spend their lives working to pay off their house, save a little for retirement, maybe even actually get out of debt. Then when the children finish high school, they find they must start all over again.

With no sign of college costs dropping, it won't be long until we find very few can afford college, if we haven't found it out already. But this country needs educated citizens to keep it running. We need engineers, statesmen, business people, and most of all, teachers. To lose students talented in these fields simply because they can't afford college is a tragedy this country can't afford.

Perhaps we could assure scholarships, fully paid scholarships, to those students who work in these fields. We have a similar plan for the military where the government pays for a college education in exchange for several years service.

If that plan is not the answer, then we all have to concentrate on finding a better plan. Otherwise we are going to end up the way Europe did in the last century, with only the elite and rich few aristocracy in charge of the economy, the government, and in control of all the lower classes. And that breeds grounds for revolution. It's why so many in Europe fled to America. It's why there was a French Revolution.

Affordable education is not just a luxury. It is a necessity for survival.

I'm Walter Furley, and that's the way I see it.

Saving Things

20 July 2007

I'm Walter Furley and this is how I see it.

Once a month a charity group comes by my house to pick up donations of items we can contribute, such as clothes, appliances, even books and magazines.

We usually have something on the front porch for them to pick up, but you know, we could give them much, much more.

We have so much *stuff* in our house, things we've collected during the forty-odd years of our marriage, much of it stored away and forgotten, but things on which we once put great sentimental value. Some just trash like old glass jars, boxes of Christmas wrapping too pretty to throw away, magazines and newspapers with articles about someone or something we found interesting. Those items are a part our lives, our history.

We recently lost a relative, and in cleaning out her house in order to sell it, we found such a vast accumulation of items that it took months to evaluate them and distribute them to various people and places where they could be used. Some reluctantly had to be put in the trash.

I suspect we all have a similar problem. Not only with the accumulation of material in our home, but a lot of unnecessary memories, worries and regrets that should have been discarded long ago. Trying to hang on to the past and trying to relive it, hoping to correct it is to deny the present and spoil the future.

In the Broadway show *Mame* there's a song called "It's Today," in which Mame throws away her disappointing past and vows to face today happy and ready for something new. Even in the musical *Annie* the song "Tomorrow" expresses the same thing.

So cleaning out a desk drawer, cleaning out a closet, even cleaning out the garage gives you a new look at what's really important in your daily life. And the things that are just a bit of a treasure, but take up just too much space, you can give away to someone who would treasure it also.

Besides, the plain fact is: if you don't clean up your place, when you're gone someone else will have to, and they may throw it all away mercilessly.

So they say that solving a problem is recognizing that it is a problem. Now for the next step.

I'm Walter Furley, and that's the way I see it.

Spider

28 July 2007

I'm Walter Furley, and this is how I see it.

Every morning this summer, and I mean *every* morning, when I go out to get the newspaper, I run into a spider web that stretches across the entrance from one shrub to another. I try to remember to wave my arms ahead of me to break the web, but I usually forget and end up with it right in my face, my eyes, and hair, requiring great effort to brush it all away.

It's the web of a little black crab spider, and I would think that after all this time, it would have realized that spinning a web there is futile. Unless it thinks there is one monstrous bug that breaks through every morning, and if he tries long enough, he will catch that big bug. Something like fishermen fishing for that monster catfish that lives in a Texas lake.

The little spider rebuilds the web very quickly. It's often there again in the afternoon and always there in the late evening waiting to ensnare me as I come and go through my front door.

The other morning I again went out to get the paper on the front lawn and once again found the spider web wrapped about my face and once again tried to brush it off. And once again kept feeling it somewhere about my head, on my ears, or in my hair.

Then as I was brushing my teeth, I saw it—the little spider was in my hair seemingly gloating as if to say, "Look, I caught it! I caught it!"

Now I am not afraid of spiders, but it made me very nervous, and I quickly brushed it out of my hair though with some difficulty. It had begun spinning a web right above my forehead. There it was on the bathroom floor, and I was ready to stomp it. But I remembered that spiders catch annoying insects like mosquitoes and gnats. So I scooped it up on a sheet of paper, opened the window, and set it free.

But I wonder what it is telling its friends about how it captured the biggest bug in the world. Like the fisherman's tale, it will be the story of the "one that got away."

There's a moral here somewhere: "Be careful what you wish for, you may get it," or "Try and try again till you succeed."

I'm sure I'll see that little spider again in the morning.

I'm Walter Furley, and that's the way I see it.

Speeding

28 August 2007

I'm Walter Furley, and this is the way I see it.

Last week my wife and I spotted a little poodle roaming the sidewalk and getting into the street. We tried to coax it into our yard, so we could pick it up and return it to its owner. But it was skittish and kept running away, finally running down a driveway as though that was where he lived. So we ended our chase.

Not five minutes later, we saw the little dog lying in the street, its head crushed and dead. We were devastated of course, but rushed to move the body out of the street.

And found a neck tag giving an address in the neighborhood. So, I drove over there and delivered the sad news, which left two ladies completely grief stricken.

The day was bright and sunny. Any observant driver would have seen that little dog in the street had he only looked, or had he not been speeding. I am assuming he was speeding, because there were no tire marks on the street nor any sign he even stopped to see what he hit. My street is a long street with no speed bumps, and there are many vehicles which speed down it much faster than necessary seemingly just for fun.

Driving vehicles too fast seems to me to be a growing problem in our society whether it is within the city or on state highways. But driving too fast in residential areas is just plain criminal.

We all need to be aware of our surroundings at all times and act accordingly. A residential street is in a neighborhood of children, a neighborhood of pets. Drivers traveling there should look for children and pets and assume they *are* going to get in your way. It's the only way to avoid them.

Drivers who drive too fast are just not relating to the world around them. They see only themselves and their vehicle, and the world better stay out of their way. We are all in this world together, and whatever you do has an effect on others, just as what they do has an effect on you. Acting in any way without responsibility is hurtful and dangerous. For everything you do there are consequences, and the consequences for driving too fast on a residential street can be tragic for your victims as well as yourself.

So I would beg everyone to get connected. You're a part of this whole neighborhood. Think of all those around you before you do anything.

If that driver last week had been aware as he drove down that residential street, he would have seen that little dog, slowed or stopped until it was out of the way, and so much grief would have been avoided. It could have been a little child running into the street, and you can imagine the excuse, "Oh, I just didn't see him." You never see unless you look.

So take the advice of the old adage, "Stop and smell the roses." Slow down and see where you are and what you're doing.

I'm Walter Furley, and that's the way I see it.

Morning Glory

30 August 2007

I'm Walter Furley, and this is how I see it.

Since my retirement, I have been delegated duties I've never had before, such as sharing housework, acting as secretary to my wife who is still working, et cetera. But the most demanding job is maintaining the landscape, in particular the hedges and the flower gardens. I've tried to keep that to a minimum, remembering to water and on occasion pull weeds, but after the recent rains it seemed a good idea to really get in there and remove all unwanted vegetation, since it should easily be pulled up from the soaked soil.

Well, I found that we were all but suffocating in morning glories. Those lovely little vines with heart shaped leaves and small purple trumpet-like blossoms. The vines were embedded in the shrubbery, on the lily stalks, on the chrysanthemums, on everything. Pulling them off was no easy matter. When you break the vines, thick sticky milk gets all over your hands, and the vines break conveniently so you can never get to the root.

And those in the taller shrubs had vines so thick, Tarzan could swing on them. It took real determination (and sweat, I might add) to remove those few I could.

I don't remember when I last tried to weed the flower beds, but these morning glory vines looked as if they had been there since creation. And since I've removed all the visible ones, I wonder how many more are lurking in the shadows or even the ground waiting to rise up and take over the garden if not the world.

It's such a shame because I used to hold them in some affection—heart shaped leaves, pale purple trumpet-like flowers. But they were just insidiously hiding behind that pretty front.

I'm sure if I go to a nursery, I can find some herbicide that will take care of them. Of course, I shall have to be very careful about applying it to avoid killing the flowers we worked so hard to grow. And I'm not so sure I am very skillful at applying poisons.

Perhaps there's a reason for morning glories in my garden. Perhaps they are there to force me to do some exercises I've avoided all these years.

But I'm warning you, morning glories, I'm watching you, and I just may come at you with a big spray gun.

I'm Walter Furley, and that's the way I see it.

My Fair Lady

9 September 2007

I'm Walter Furley, and this is how I see it.

Harbor Playhouse has another success on its hands in this latest production of *My Fair Lady*. It is one of the most produced musicals in amateur theater, and this production tells you why. First, get some good singers to sing the songs, and even with a small orchestra, add to that some imaginative sets (and *My Fair Lady* has an abundance of scene changes), some positively lavish costumes, some very imaginative and amusing dancing, and you have a production that transcends anything expected of a local theater.

Especially pleasing is the Eliza, Monica Flores. Her bright, clear voice soars out over the theater in every one of her songs, delightfully so. Pet Lutz as Higgins was just right as the blustering, egotistical professor who transforms the flower girl into a lady. But be greatly surprised at the lavish costumes. The Ascot scene was filled with enough Victorian designer gowns to make you gasp in wonder. And then, the ballroom scene has some of the most beautiful and colorful costumes ever put on the Harbor Playhouse stage. It all added up to one delightful evening. Director Joel Earley made the most of this show, just as he did with *Oklahoma* last month.

Presenting shows such as this on the shoestring budget that local theaters must work with, means the theater relies on community support to keep operating. I urge you to make very effort to see this show. It will encourage you to see more of the coming productions and insure the continuing operation of one of our city's cultural assets.

This past week Harbor Playhouse lost one of its most loyal patrons. Alice Gabbard passed away at her residence on Thursday. She had supported the theater with her talent as an actress, with her wisdom as a board member, and her money as a generous donor. The theater dedicated Saturday night's performance to her memory. Alice Gabbard loved a good show, and she would have loved this Harbor Playhouse production of *My Fair Lady*.

I'm Walter Furley, and that is how I see it.

Cell Phones

19 September 2007

I'm Walter Furley, and this is how I see it.

Cell phones are either the greatest invention of all time or the worst.

I'm ambivalent because I feel comfort in knowing I can reach my family members anytime no matter where they are. Yet I'm irritated to have a perfect stranger stand right next to me and speak in an unusually loud voice to a small plastic box stuck to his ear. Or I might say, "her ear."

Just the other day I was picking out tomatoes at the grocery store when an athletic-looking man said quite firmly, "Hi." Naturally, I responded with a smile and "Hi" of my own, expecting him to be someone I must know. But no. He glared at me and mouthed silently, "I'm on the phone!" And looked at me as if I had intruded on his space. He continued the conversation on the phone a little further away, but still very audible to all near him. It was impossible not to listen boring as the conversation was. He was having trouble coordinating picking up his kids after school as well as doing grocery shopping.

Were I to use a cell phone (I so far have refused to get one), I think I would seek out a place of some solitude so as not to disturb others and to keep my conversation private.

It's my wife who has our family cell phone, and she insists you have to talk loudly to be heard by the person calling. But some of those phones are so loud, you can hear both the caller and the called.

In restaurants, I have heard business deals being made at tables twenty feet away. And those using the phone not only ignore the presence of the many other customers dining, but seem even proud of using the phone in this manner. I think they want the rest of us to hear them and make us think, "Boy, he must be somebody important!" We don't.

But, it's a free country. We can use our cell phones anyway we want, but those phones seem to be battling down just one more bastion guarding our civility. As in all things human, cell phones should be used in consideration of all those around them. None of us should be forced to hear people right next us conversing as if we didn't exist.

Can you hear me now?

I'm Walter Furley, and that's the way I see it.

Mess with Texas

28 September 2007

I'm Walter Furley, and this is how I see it.

This week, I was driving down the street, when out of the vehicle in front of me came a paper bag and a big plastic drinking cup, complete with straw. What's more, there was a "Don't Mess with Texas" sign along the street.

I should have stopped my car and picked up the trash immediately, but traffic was heavy, and there was no room to pull over.

But I regarded the trash as a direct insult. The driver must have seen me behind him as well as all the other cars in the traffic. He just didn't care. It wasn't his street.

But it was. It is. We're all living here in this city, this country, this world together. But he just didn't feel a part of it.

Disregarding the feelings and rights of others is a dehumanizing attitude. Throwing trash on our streets or on our beaches is as bad as throwing trash on our yards.

There's a neighbor in my part of town that has won "Yard of the Month" at least twice. It is such a pleasure to drive by and see the neatly trimmed lawn, the blooming flower beds, and the well cared for trees. But that yard didn't get that way naturally. It took hard work to prepare the flower beds, to keep the lawn green and evenly mowed, and the trees well trimmed and fertilized.

To have someone drive down that street and carelessly throw out a sandwich bag or other trash would be a sacrilege, a real wound to the beauty of the neighborhood.

I am always reassured when driving down highways that are neatly maintained and feel grateful when I see a sign that says "This highway kept clean by..." some organization like the 4H Club or even employees of a company. Those people feel connected. They feel the highway is just as important as their front yard or even their living room.

The people who throw trash don't feel the connection. And I suspect would be willing to insult me to my face if I suggested they not throw trash. They treat people the same way they treat the world around them. They really don't care about much of anything.

It's the caring that makes this world beautiful. It's the caring that makes us human.

Perhaps we should change the state's motto to "Let's care about Texas."

When you throw trash onto our landscape, you are making yourself less a part of civilization, less a part of humanity.

When you mess with Texas, you are really messing with yourself.

I'm Walter Furley, and that's the way I see it.

Smiles

11 October 2007

I'm Walter Furley, and this is how I see it.

I read a curious article the other day.

According to it you can control your brain and your attitude with your face. Yes. It said if you are feeling glum or discontented, if you will just smile, you will immediately feel better. The muscles in your face make your brain respond to whatever expression you are making and make you feel accordingly.

Well, I tried it—a bright smile as though something wonderful had just happened. And you know what? It worked.

I could feel my cheeks relaxing and forming a nice, round ball on each side of my face, my lips were turned up as though they were ready to laugh, and whatever I was thinking beforehand just disappeared.

So I tested it in reverse. I forced a frown, and immediately the thoughts about the hot weather, the high cost of gasoline, and the many little jobs I had to do, all came tumbling back into my head.

So I went back to smiling. And I immediately remembered a happy moment when some relatives visited us and the fun we had.

But I still doubted it. This was just too simple. Life is more complicated than this. A smile is not going to increase my bank balance or trim those hedges, or fix the car. But a smile does make the jobs easier.

Frowning and worrying only make things worse. The article said smiling took only a few muscles, while frowning took many more and much more effort. Frowning is hard work. Smiling is easy.

So I think I'll go ahead and look a little stupid with an enigmatic smile. And if anyone asks me why I've got a silly grin on my face, I'll tell them, "It feels good."

I'm Walter Furley, and that's the way I see it.

Deodorant

15 October 2007

I'm Walter Furley, and this is how I see it.

My wife and I were shopping recently, when a gentleman passed us by who had obviously not bathed in a few days or at least had not used his deodorant in some time. Now that is unusual, you must admit, though on a recent visit to England, I noticed, especially in elevators, several people did not believe in deodorants.

But I got to thinking, when did we decide that the smell of honest sweat was so offensive. I remember my father coming in from working in the fields on our little farm with a nice salty, sweaty smell. And in school, quite often by the end of recess, some of us were a little redolent. But so what?

I was born during the Great Depression, and our house did not have running water. Water was collected in a cistern and carried by buckets into the kitchen for use. So family baths were a real effort and usually done on Saturday night so we would be nice and clean for Sunday school and church. The children were all bathed in one tub of water set in the middle of the large kitchen. The smallest of us bathed first, then the next smallest, and on up to me as the last to use the one tub of water. Actually we boys liked to be last because that meant the last one could relieve himself into the bathwater, one of our major entertainments. But during the week, washing body parts was limited to hands and face and feet, since going barefoot was a way of life then. I'm sure that during the week we developed some sort of body odor. Clothes had to be worn more than once before wash day. And I can't remember anyone finding any smell to be objectionable.

It must have been those radio commercials that educated us. Remember something called "Mum"? It was a white cream in a small jar smelling of some sort of spice or herb. Its smell was certainly detectable and maybe more offensive than regular body odor.

But it immediately made body odor a social no-no and left all us smelly people ostracized and subject to ridicule, if not to our faces then certainly behind our backs.

Remember that commercial, "Aren't you glad you use Dial, don't you wish everybody did?"

Now, deodorants are not only expected, but required for any social intercourse. Indeed, we men are expected to go the extra mile with expensive colognes and after shaves.

Have you noticed how much sales space is taken up in department stores for men's colognes? And the cost? Most around fifty dollars. Those colognes are banned in our church choir, for many people are actually allergic to the oils used in the scents. The ladies tell us men to avoid the colognes, but deodorants are all right.

The gentleman who passed me in the store may have not had time to bathe that morning, or no one to launder his clothes so he had clean garments every day, or maybe he wasn't aware of his odor. Or maybe he just didn't care. And that's his right. There are certainly worse things that smelling a little stale. We all do at one time or another. We just try not to do it in public.

I'm Walter Furley, and that's the way I see it.

Cell Tones

24 November 2007

I'm Walter Furley, and this is how I see it.

I was completely taken aback recently in a public place, when a terrifying sound of a Tarzan yell came in my immediate proximity. But then I heard a casual "hello" and realized it came from a cell phone.

Other cell phones I have heard bellow out a rock and roll song or some startling sound effect, all nothing like the friendly ringing of a telephone. Some phones do play music. I like, such as "Eine Kleine Nachtmusik" or Handel's "Water Music," but all completely inappropriate for a telephone ring.

Why do the cell phone holders do that? They can control what they want their rings to sound like. Why don't they choose something less offensive? Do they want to bring to the world's attention that they have a cell phone all their own and demonstrate they can do with it any thing they wish? If so, the message has been received, so over and out, and go back to a simple telephone ring that does not bother those nearby.

Surely they have thought of the possibility of their forgetting to turn off the phone, say at a movie or a symphony concert or a church service, and suddenly a Tarzan yell disturbs the entire hemisphere with a volume so high it could send those nearby into a nervous collapse.

Such conveniences as cell phones should be unobtrusive, used in hushed undertones if not in private. Having to hear a loud tinny rendition of the "Stars and Stripes Forever" in a restaurant, or heaven forbid, an elevator is an offensive invasion of what young people call "my space," and I resent it. Don't force me to hear and react to your disturbing cell phone rings and expect me to ignore your very private conversation. Keep your distance, stay in your space, and leave me alone in mine.

I'm Walter Furley, and that's the way I see it.

To See the World

30 November 2007

I'm Walter Furley, and this is how I see it.

I reread one my favorite poems recently, "Auguries of Innocence" by William Blake and marveled at the very first verse:

> To see the world in a grain of sand,
> Heaven in a wild flower,
> Hold infinity in the palm of your hand,
> Eternity in an hour.

It reminds me that every little thing is just a part of something much, much greater—the grain of sand on the beach, the flower that has been growing each season since time began. And I can't help but be filled with wonder at how it all evolves so perfectly. The sand tumbles to and fro, grinding each grain down smaller and smaller. The flower goes to seed and blooms again each year.

Yet where do I come in?

I have tried to trace my genealogy but can go no further back than three generations. And while all those seem to have been fine, upstanding citizens, I wonder about those before them. Thomas Wolfe had a line in one of his novels that said he was here because a London cutpurse went unhung. Some of our ancestors must have survived the plague, perhaps fought in the Crusades, a minute part of momentous historical events. Some may even have been the illegitimate offspring of kings. Whatever they were, here I am, a result of their lives, like a link in a chain on which hangs all civilization.

So what? I enjoy the seashore, walking on the ancient sand. I smell the flowers that were gathered by strangers millennia ago. A guest in a world that was made by others and filled with their inventions and ideas all delivered as a gift to me. Surely I am expected, even obligated, to leave something here to make sure it all continues. But what remains a mystery. I'll never be a Copernicus and solve the mystery of the universe or Thomas Edison and invent marvelous things. I hope it's enough to keep my part of the world neat, and smile at those I meet, and have the grace to admire and congratulate those who can do more than I. As a result of all that has been, and a part of all that is to come, at least I can try to do no harm. And take my place beside the grain of sand and the wild flower.

I'm Walter Furley, and that's the way I see it.

2008

Joshua Bell

10 January 2008

I'm Walter Furley, and this is how I see it.

I was fortunate enough to attend the Corpus Christi Symphony's concert featuring Joshua Bell the first of the year.

He and his Stradivarius violin lived up to all the hype and then some. He could hold you spellbound as he played music high as the stratosphere and so softly you had to lean on the edge of your seat to hear it or with such a gusto you were knocked back in your seat by his intense energy. All of it beautiful music played with superb control and skill.

His biography said he is some forty years old now after making a professional debut at fourteen. Joshua Bell has a tremendous repertoire memorized, likely every violin concerto ever written along with all the solo show pieces. He has a youthful athletic look about him. Indeed he is said to be a fine tennis player and defies musician convention by refusing to wear tuxedo or tails while performing. Instead he wore black trousers tailored like slim-cut jeans and a black long sleeved shirt, likely silk, with a satin trim down the front, leaving his neck and shoulder open for placing his priceless Stradivarius violin.

Women, of course, wear dresses that leave their neck and shoulders free for the instrument, but men have been bound by a high-collared shirt and thick coat which must be a hindrance. Joshua Bell may have started a new costume tradition among concert violinists.

But my fascination with his performance was tempered by the thought of the lifetime of preparation for this concert and his career. Every day has to include hours of practice, hours you and I might spend in housework, yardwork, or the movies, or even enjoying radio and TV.

Joshua Bell has to keep ever ready to perform, whether in recording studios, or in concert halls all over the world. I once read a quote from the pianist Paderewski saying, "If I miss one day's practice, I can tell it. If I miss two days practice, my audience can tell it." His entire life is controlled by concert engagements, most of which require travel time to places all over the world. You must wonder, do such artists ever have any free time to do absolutely nothing. Being a professional musician requires real commitment, dedication, and the sacrifice of many things you and I take for granted.

So I am grateful to the artists who accept their gifts of talent and spend their lives to perfect them just for our enjoyment and inspiration. They prove there are goals and standards for each of us that can be reached if we work at it.

I'm Walter Furley, and that's the way I see it.

Texas Fall

10 January 2008

I'm Walter Furley and this is how I see it.

I have relatives who live in upstate New York, in the Adirondacks, and they E-mail me pictures of the heavy snows this time of year, with the children out playing in it, knowing that our temperatures this time of year can be in the seventies with many sunny days.

But it's January, and my trees have just now shed all their leaves making this our autumn. Yet, the bulb flowers are sprouting and will be blooming within weeks anticipating spring by a month or so. Lawns that are watered are still green, and it takes a real north wind to make us wear a coat or jacket or even long sleeves. To my northern relatives, we are in a perpetual summer.

Yet the naked trees remind us the season has changed; the world is another year older, as are we. While it would be nice to see a neighborhood with tall red and yellow trees, it is also nice not to have to rake up the masses of fallen leaves. And while we would enjoy looking out over a city covered in snow, we do not have to face the muddy mess the melting snow would leave.

I once read an article that claimed all of history's great ideas and inventions have come from the cold countries. We in the tropics or subtropics have contributed little to the improvement of civilization, according to the article. The only inventions I can recall from the Sunbelt are the cotton gin and computers in Silicon Valley, though I'm sure there are many more. If Copernicus had lived in Texas instead of cold, wintry Poland, would he have discovered that earth revolved around the sun, instead of vice versa? He just might have been out enjoying the sunshine and beaches instead of being confined to a dark room in a house covered with ice and snow, and it would be years before we realized the sun was not moving across the sky with a sun god driving it. But I'm sure NASA in Houston would have noticed sooner or later.

But my point is: we each live where we like and like where we live. Snow lovers make their choices; we sun lovers make ours. And it is no small matter that many of those snow lovers are spending the snow season right here in sunny South Texas.

Still it would be pleasant to spend a summer in the Adirondacks, especially knowing the winter would be in Corpus Christi.

I'm Walter Furley, and that's how I see it.

Aunt

22 January 2008

I'm Walter Furley, and this is how I see it.

I try so hard *not* to get annoyed when I hear someone refer to a relative as "Ahnt."

Growing up in Texas, it was always Ant Nellie, Ant Catherine, Ant Velma. Of course we spelled it A-U-N-T, but we saw no reason to include the *u* in the pronunciation. So when I hear other Texans or Southerners say "Ahnt Mary," I sense a sort of snobbishness. They all know the word is *Ant*. We even stress it more when we say, "An-tie." We would never say "Ahn-tie."

Of course, that is a regional pronunciation, and I have to forgive those who live elsewhere who learned to say "Ahnt" and would never say "Ant." Now when we Texans speak of the little stinging insect, whose name is spelled a-n-t without the u, we diphthong the vowel to a-yunt. And we know decidedly the difference between ant and a-yunt.

And we have our own pronunciation of other words on which newcomers are trying to correct us. An obvious one is the town of Refugio—pronounced re-FUR-ry-oh by the natives, re-FEW-he-o by the Spanish purists.

Or Falfurrias, also a Spanish name, but called fal-FUR-ry-us by us who live here. And we raise an eyebrow to those who try to correct us with fahl-FOO-ry-us.

Spanish names have a legitimate claim to be pronounced with the Spanish rules, and it would behoove us to recognize them as such and pronounce them that way.

But Ahnt? I know the Websters gives ahnt as first choice, with ant a mere second. But tradition dies hard.

Several years ago my dear Aunt Edith visited from England with a young English cousin. The eight-year-old cousin began addressing her as Ant Edith, and Ant Edith corrected her. "It is AHNT Edith," she said. The little cousin said, "But everyone here in Texas calls you Ant Edith," to which Ant Edith replied, "Yes, dear, but they don't know better." That is not exactly true. We do know better. We just choose to be true to Texas traditions.

I'm Walter Furley, and that is how I see it.

TV

24 January 2008

I'm Walter Furley, and this is how I see it.

I confess to enjoying TV sitcoms. Most of them are well acted, have likable characters, who do much to amuse me. But...

I am getting more and more concerned about the shows' reliance on sexual situations for humor. The basic premise is: sex is fun, and any and everybody can enjoy it, married or not. And that is a truth we cannot deny. But the comedies seem to make sex a casual thing like eating ice cream with no consequences and no compunctions. No one gets pregnant, no one gets diseases, and no one gets a broken heart. Those things aren't funny. But they are also a truth we cannot deny.

My concern would be of no consequence if all this were confined to television screens. But those screens seem to be reflecting real life. Too many young viewers are seeing these characters as role models and behaving like them in real life. And the real consequences are divorce, unwanted pregnancies, diseases, and heartbreak. It takes a strong family to instill the values of honesty, loyalty, and responsibility in children. It would seem that the writers of these comedies do not have those values. Going for the big laugh in a show may pay off in the ratings, but if it trivializes sex as a casual entertainment and not a profound expression of love, then it is misleading us all into thinking commitment and responsibility are really not all that important. I shall continue to laugh at the comedies but remind myself these actors are playing fools, behaving foolishly, and that's why they are funny. They are not role models. They are fools, and no one wants to be a fool.

I'm Walter Furley, and that's the way I see it.

Academy Awards

26 January 2008

I'm Walter Furley, and this is how I see it.

I really enjoy movies. Sitting in a darkened theater with the surround sound enveloping you, one can really get lost in a story or even another world and feel you personally know some brand new characters created by writers, directors, and actors.

So I like to watch at the end of the season which artists are chosen as best and see if the choice agrees with mine. Usually they do.

But the spectacle is watching the actors parade down the red carpet wearing the latest fashions, some beautiful, some outrageous, but all interesting.

The irony of the whole event is the best movies and best performances are rarely the ones that make the most money, which means only a limited audience sees the winners.

For instance, Halle Berry won best actress for *Monsters Ball.*

Can you name anyone who has seen *Monsters Ball?*

So the Academy Awards is reduced to a display very similar to a dog show by the American Kennel Club. The various actors parade before the cameras to be judged by the audience, who mentally award blue ribbons for best of breed and best show. And the cutest and most beautiful and most handsome and funniest and most publicized actors and movies rake in the money.

But the movie producers know this. It is brave of them to persist in making good movies, even though they aren't always blockbusters.

And that means that I can count on sitting in a darkened theater, getting fascinated by some engrossing photography, overcome by some marvelous acting and story, and literally surrounded by music and sound effects for an experience found nowhere else but in a movie theater. I should amend my opening statement that I really enjoy movies. I really enjoy good movies.

I'm Walter Furley, and that's the way I see it.

Entertainment

31 January 2008

I'm Walter Furley, and this is how I see it.

I'm appalled at how the entertainment industry is influencing our very lives. The hair style you are wearing is likely the one some actor or singer wears when performing. The clothes you wear are likely in the style of some performer, especially among the young people. Our language uses words made up by a performer in a comedy routine or a recording. The Rap performers have used obscenities so often in their recordings that such words are in everyday language among some people, at least. Some words that were once unprintable, or printed with an initial and three hyphens, are now appearing in some of our best magazines. Movie or television story lines place characters in situations that were once considered too racy to even talk about. Remember when Mary Tyler Moore and Dick Van Dyke could use only separate beds even though they were a charming married couple?

And much of newscasts is given over to people in the entertainment industry, as though a national story should tell us who is dating who, and what sensational dress an actress dared to wear in public.

The awards ceremonies have become some of televisions highest rated shows. And those entertainers often offer their personal advice on politics, on diets and health, sexual relationships, and even religion. Most of these people are self-centered spending their lives seeking fame and fortune and have very little interest in you and me except as paying customers to their shows. Their life styles have little in common with yours and mine, and they quite frequently break all the traditions and mores on which most civilizations have been built.

I'll grant that there are exceptions. Some are model citizens and hold the same values as most of the rest of us. My favorite is Paul Newman whose charity work is phenomenal.

But the influence of many is eroding the basic fabric of society as we know it. People appear in public in what was once underwear. People behave rudely and crudely as they have seen rock stars do. Worst of all, the use of drugs by so-called celebrities has become attractive to so many people that they imitate those stars with fatal results.

If so many look to the entertainment world to set our standards, the entertainment world has a responsibility to set those standards high. You who have won our attention and admiration, you owe us something in return. A respect for the values that have made us a civil society thus far.

I'm Walter Furley, and that's the way I see it.

Observing Life

11 February 2008

I'm Walter Furley, and this is how I see it.

I was driving down the street I always take when going to town and noticed a new shop that had opened up. But my wife pointed out that the shop had been there some time, and I was just now noticing it.

That was disturbing. Being in the news business, I always thought I was more observant of my surroundings. Indeed I thought I could testify as a witness to some event because I saw it all. But now that I'm retired, my powers of observance must be retired also.

I suspect we all ignore much of what lies along our usual pathways. We go on automatic pilot and think of other things until we reach a stoplight or hit a pothole. I'm not talking about being an alert driver or failing to be one. I'm talking about seeing the world about you.

As I drive down Ocean Drive, I enjoy looking at the water. In the morning it seems to be a deep blue, at noon almost white or gray, and at evening a shade of green. An artist friend pointed that out to me once, and I've always checked to see what the color the bay is as I drive by.

Artists do seem to have a sharper eye that the rest of us. They see the gradations of color and light in everything and think what paint they would use to put what they see into a picture.

We don't have to be that expert. It's enough to just see how blue the sky is today, the shape of the clouds, the especially beautiful trees that decorate our city, the beautiful yards that many neighbors have spent hours cultivating, the thousands of birds that often rest on our power lines. There is so much to see!

Not all of it beautiful, of course. There is trash that lines some streets or floats in our bay, stray pets darting dangerously into traffic, inattentive drivers who endanger us. Being aware of what's going on could keep you out of trouble and help you make the world a better place like cleaning up trash or saving a lost pet. Being aware of others could alert you to someone in need or someone who just wants a smile, like your grocery check-out clerk.

Being aware is part of being alive. Just look around you. As I said, there is so much to see.

I'm Walter Furley, and that's the way I see it.

Rhythm of Life

11 February 2008

I'm Walter Furley, and this is the way I see it.

I was pleasantly startled to see the ornamental pear trees in bloom this morning. There is a spectacular one on Alameda and a small grove of them on Santa Fe on Lamar Park. They all bloom at once, last about a week, and then turn green for the rest of the year.

I've noticed that when my hibiscus blooms, hibiscus are blooming all over the city, as though some secret signal has been sent from somewhere alerting the bushes that it is time to bloom. The same with the pink hawthorn, though they seem to be late this year.

How do these plants know when to bloom? While they do bloom as spring approaches, there is always some variance in the timing. Is it a matter of just the right temperature, just the right amount of sunshine, just the right amount of rain, or all of the above?

I like to think there is some mystical force out there deciding when it is time to bloom, and as the time arrives, something like a radio frequency is broadcast, and all the plants get the message and burst forth in beautiful blossoms.

There are solunar tables that predict activity among animal life, that show the times when birds are hopping about and feeding, when fish and animals like deer are most active and more easily caught. That indicates there is some rhythm in nature that affects animal and plant life. Does it also affect us humans?

We all know good days and bad days, but blame it on diet or exercise or lack thereof. Could it be we also are receiving signals that say "Get up and get going," or "Take it easy today"? And do we all get the same signals at the same time?

I'm sure the astrologists could offer an explanation, but the horoscopes I read in the paper all seem so general that they apply to me, no matter what sign they are written for.

Yet there is something intriguing about the fact that when one hibiscus blooms, they all bloom. When birds are hopping about looking for food, birds are hopping about everywhere. They all seem to know, "It's time!"

The idea is perfectly good excuse to nap. When you feel the signal, you should obey Mother Nature and just take a nice rest. I get those signals all the time.

I'm Walter Furley, and that's the way I see it.

Lost Keys

8 March 2008

I'm Walter Furley, and this is how I see it.

We depend on too many small "things" to run our lives.

I recently misplaced my keys, a key ring holding my car keys, my wife's car keys, my house keys, my safety deposit key, and two keys to something I've completely forgotten about. But there I was, with no access to my house or my car. Luckily I had a duplicate car key for emergency use, but without that jangle in my pocket, I felt lost and helpless. I had to ring the door bell like some visitor to be let into the house. If I drove my wife's car, I had to have her keys, which left her in the same predicament as I.

I spent hours going over my routine of the day, remembering when I last used the keys, and always ended up with the fact that they must be in the house…somewhere. But where? Time I should have been using to plan other things was wasted on worrying about the location of those keys. I even called the restaurant we used that day, but they had no keys for me. I cleaned out the seats and floors of both cars, searching under seats—which is impossible to access, by the way; you just can't get under the seats of these new cars—looked under beds, chairs, sofas, even went through trash cans, to no avail.

After two days of frustration, borrowing my wife's keys and forgetting to return them to her, I was ready to go the expense of getting all duplicates. But in a last desperate act of searching I moved a stack of books I had been rearranging, and there were the keys. Such a weight was lifted, such relief. I was a whole person again, not dependent on someone else to admit me to my own house and give me a needed ride. All because of a metal ring holding a half dozen keys. As a youth, I grew up in a time when no one thought of locking their house, and the family car was driven only by my father. I had to walk anywhere I wanted to go. I almost wished I could return to that time. We run our lives now with keys. Or do the keys run our lives for us? The fact is, we can't do much without them.

I'm Walter Furley, and that's the way I see it.

Street Sweeping

16 March 2008

I'm Walter Furley, and this is how I see it.

One of the stories I remember about the famous recording artist Freddy Fender told of how he proudly moved his mother from Mexico to a house on Ocean Drive. And the first morning after she moved there, Freddy said he saw her out sweeping the driveway and her part of Ocean Drive, just the way she had swept her own yard and street in Mexico. He said he had to explain to her that sweeping the street was not done in America.

And I began thinking, "Well, it should be." I and my neighbors sweep our sidewalks often, but never the street unless something unusual ends up there. What a cleaner neighborhood, what a cleaner world it would be if everyone kept his part of it swept clean and neat.

It is likely inadvisable to sweep Ocean Drive, even if you live there, what with all the traffic there. But what's to keep us from keeping clean the streets in our neighborhood? The mechanical street cleaner does not come around that often. And to be really responsible and "green," when we go walking, why not carry a little trash bag to pick the stray bits of trash that end up along the way? There is a man who lives in Trinity Towers who does that and even does it as he walks his dog.

We cannot stop some people from "messing with Texas" and throwing trash from their cars all over the landscape. While we can see such trash often, rarely do we see the people who throw it.

So, if we take responsibility for disposing of what trash we see whether it's on our own property or not, we will have done our duty to protect some part of the environment.

Freddy Fender's mother set us all a fine example. Keep your part of the world swept clean and neat.

I'm Walter Furley, and that's the way I see it.

Charlton Heston

7 April 2008

I'm Walter Furley, and this is how I see it.

I was saddened to hear of the death of Charlton Heston just recently.

He had been ill for sometime and had made no films in years, but somehow I thought he would always be with us. And it reminds me of just how ephemeral are the performing arts. His work in films will be seen and appreciated as long as there is film or tape to record it. But the work of actors and musicians in theaters or concert halls last only for the moment they are performing. However moved you are by what you see and hear them do, that performance ends with the final curtain and can live only in your memory.

I've read reviews of the work of people such as John Barrymore, Franz Liszt, Caruso, all called great by their contemporaries. But we have to trust those who saw and heard them and wrote about them.

The artists we see in our lifetime like Joshua Bell and Rene Fleming pour out their hearts in performances. We see and applaud them, and they hear the applause and are surely grateful. But the performance is gone, and there was just that hour or so, or maybe only a moment, when we are moved and touched and know something beautiful we've never known before and may never know again.

And you wonder, why do people dedicate their lives to learning to perform this? Do they spend their lives in training just to create that one beautiful moment of connection with an audience? Ballet dancers must surely be possessed to discipline their bodies so rigorously that they literally wear them out after just a few years of performing. And when those artists pass on, all that is left is the memories or the descriptions written of their work.

Thank goodness the artists and performers don't think of the time when they're gone. They live for that magical moment when they can reveal to us the wonderful sights and sounds that life has to offer.

Thank you Charlton Heston and all who have gone before you.

I'm Walter Furley, and that is how I see it.

Volunteer

7 April 2008

I'm Walter Furley, and this is how I see it.

I found out something about our city the other day to which I had given very little thought. The city maintains a very active Volunteer Services program. Thousands of people here in Corpus Christi donate, give away, their time and effort to help other people. And the city's Volunteer department helps match the people who need help with those who want to give help.

The biggest department is the RSVP services which let retired seniors register showing what talents and abilities they have to be matched up with the very persons needing those talents and abilities.

One group specializes in building ramps into houses where handicapped people live but cannot get down steps. I've seen those people building those steps but assumed they were hired professional carpenters. But they were people working to build the ramps for free. Others act as mentors to at-risk youths, helping them in school studies. Some make hospital visits to those who have no family to help them or even visit and chat with them. Some teach English to immigrants; some volunteer to help people recover from natural disasters like fires and floods. There seems to be no limit as to how one could help out his neighbors and no limit as the neighbors who need help.

One program is called Senior Companions, volunteers to commit themselves to helping elderly or handicapped people living alone with no family to turn to. Twice a week they come visiting, just to sit and chat with the seniors or help with grocery shopping or the simple daily tasks the residents are unable to do for themselves. And you'd be surprised at the number of older adults who have no one to help or even visit them. These Senior Companions help the home-bound remain independent to live in their own homes. If you can be a volunteer, just call city hall and ask for the Volunteer Services department, and they will fix you up. It's amazing how many people and organizations need volunteers. There are even volunteers who help out here at KEDT.

The real benefit though is the wonderful personal feeling you get from helping out. You make so many new friends you would never meet otherwise. While those you help appreciate you, it's you who get the real pleasure.

I'm Walter Furley, and that is how I see it.

Greetings

16 April 2008

I'm Walter Furley, and this is how I see it.

Do you ever stop and think about how we greet people? We usually say "Hi, how are you?" And the other person responds, "Fine, how are you?" And you may say, "Great!" and go on with a conversation or pass on by. But you have each asked a very probing question, "How are you?" And to really answer, you'd have to list a lingering headache, sore feet, an upcoming operation, a disturbing situation at work—everything that would tell just how you are. So, do we really want to know "How are you?" Of course we are concerned by our friend's general welfare, but to express it in a casual greeting seems inappropriate.

I like to be greeted with, "Hi, good to see you!" Then I can answer, "You too!" Or maybe, "Hi, you look great today!" And they may say "Thanks" or "So do you" or maybe not. Not all of us look great all the time, though we like to be told we do.

Of course, if you really want to know about how people are, you can get specific and say "Hi, I haven't seen you in so long. Are you all right?" Then you can stand and listen to the problems with the children, the failure of a diet, the escalating price of gasoline, and on and on. But be prepared to get a real list of griefs and have a lot of empathy to offer. You are committing yourself to an intense visit of several minutes, if not hours.

So, I propose we eliminate a greeting of "How are you?" when it's a brief passing or casual meeting and limit it to a real and honest greeting of "Good morning," or "Great to see you," or "You look terrific." (Though *terrific* sounds great, it really means "you are terrifying.")

But being specific in what we say takes careful thought, and that is a rare trait today. So perhaps it is enough to utter nonsensical phrases in a friendly manner.

I once met a stranger in an elevator and said to him, "Hello, how are you?" And he replied "Fantastic!" in a voice so loud, it almost knocked me down. It left me speechless and ever since has made me think before I say "How are you?"

I'm Walter Furley, and that is how I see it.

Leadership

16 April 2008

I'm Walter Furley, and this is how I see it.

I sincerely hope you saw and heard the last concert of the Corpus Christi Symphony. There was a fantastic fourteen year old boy who played the Rachmaninoff concerto so brilliantly, he had the entire audience on its feet jumping and cheering—very exciting!

But then the orchestra combined with a number of choirs to perform Orff's *Carmina Burana*, which also brought a prolonged ovation. What a satisfying evening. And it came to mind that this is a perfect example of what fine leadership can achieve. The many people performing were doing so because they had a great desire to do so. But they needed someone to show them how and to bring together the stage full of performers.

The several choirs spent hours with their individual directors studying and practicing the scores, then in the days prior to the performance worked with a renowned director, Dr. Ronald Shirey, to get them all to the same level of performance. The orchestra of course spent hours in rehearsal to prepare, and then all the participants were united under the direction of Maestro John Giordano. And what a task faced him. The orchestra was larger than usual seeming to fill the entire stage. And the choir must have had nearly two hundred singers, stretching from wall to wall of the Performing Arts Center. And the maestro had to grab the attention and concentration of every person on that stage and hold it for the forty-five minutes it took to perform that work.

And grab them all, he did. We could feel the electricity vibrating between him and every person on that stage. And *Carmina Burana* is a very difficult work. The words are in Latin, the rhythms are complex, and the dynamics are changing from minute to minute. There could be no letdown in concentration by anyone. The result was just glorious. And it occurred to me, if only we as ordinary citizens could devote that much energy and concentration to the governing of our nation or of the world, how very much could be achieved. Of course, we would need leaders who could inspire us to our goals, and we would need to unite in our efforts and commit ourselves to achieving those goals just the way those performers did at the Symphony concert.

A consummation devoutly to be wished. If only…

I"m Walter Furley, and that's how I see it.

Washington's Death

29 April 2008

I'm Walter Furley, and this is how I see it.

I love to go to book stores and just look, if not read. And I always end up at the bargain tables where thirty-dollar books are now down to five dollars or less. They all were published two and three years ago, but are still good books.

The latest I chose was a great biography of George Washington by a writer named Willard Stearne Randall. It is very detailed, especially about the many battles Washington was involved in with the French, the Indians, and finally the British. But I was amazed at the medical practices at that time just over two hundred years ago. Washington was apparently prone to upper respiratory infections or the flu, and it was this which afflicted him when he died. The author says Washington had a cold but insisted on riding out in a snow storm to inspect his farm property on December 13,1799. He returned to Mount Vernon, soaking wet, cold (it was 28 degrees that day) and went directly to the dinner table without changing insisting he was all right but did complain of a sore throat. When Martha insisted he take some herbal medicine, he refused, saying he never took anything for a cold, but always let it go as it came.

But by morning he complained of a very sore throat, could hardly talk, and had Martha send for some of his staff. They persuaded Washington to send for a doctor, but until he arrived, Washington asked his assistant to bleed him. That is cut an artery and drain an amount of blood, a common medical practice at the time. Martha begged him not to do that, but Washington insisted. When the doctor arrived, he applied something called Spanish Fly to Washington's throat, which raised a blister, so they bled him again. He tried to gargle with sage tea and vinegar and almost choked, so he was bled again. And everyone wondered why he was growing weaker by the moment.

During the morning, two more doctors arrived, diagnosed the problem as acute tonsillitis, or quinsy, and prescribed more blisters and purgatives, and bled him again. One of the doctors was a young man, who had just returned from medical school in Scotland, and he protested the bleeding and prescribed a radical new technique to help Washington breathe, a tracheotomy. But the older doctors refused the idea, and bled the president again. Well, of course Washington was dead by the afternoon.

This treatment was practiced just two hundred years ago. Our medicine today is quite new in the history of man, and we can only wonder how our ancestors could have been so stupid as to believe bleeding a person's life blood could save his life.

We can wonder at the marvelous buildings of the ancient world, the beautiful art and sculpture created then, but medicine is something we have just begun to understand in the past few generations. And thankfully we are learning more every day. Just makes you wonder, what were the good old days?

I'm Walter Furley, and that is how I see it.

Harp Music

30 April 2008

I am Walter Furley, and this is how I see it.

Harp music is more than just music; it is a mental massage. Just as a masseuse can tone up your muscles and leave you calm and relaxed, so does harp music massage the mind.

I was so fortunate to be able to persuade a beautiful girl who played the harp to marry me. I get to hear harp music every day of my life. And it is easy for me to attribute all the good things in my life to hearing that music every day.

When you are near a harp playing, those strings are vibrating the air about you, and those vibrations enter your hearing, reach your brain, and just sort things out. They bring an order to your thoughts.

And there's no reason to believe those harp vibrations don't affect your body, soothing your muscles, erasing tensions, and calming you all over.

No wonder King Saul asked David to play the harp for him, though I wonder if David's harp sounded as soothing as harps made today.

I've read articles by physicians who bring harpists to play in hospital wards, especially for terminal patients, and those doctors say they can see a marked improvement in the physical status of those who are so ill. A harpist friend in San Antonio has been asked to play in operating rooms while surgery is actually underway. She has to wear scrubs, a cap and a mask, but her hands are free to play the harp.

And the surgeons and nurses say they benefit from the sounds, as well as the patient, who is anesthetized of course but is still in the presence of the soothing vibrations of the harp.

I enjoy hearing recorded harp music, especially the masters who have such expert technique, but the physical benefit is not the same.

To be in the proximity of a harp being played is just plain good therapy both physically and mentally. The perfectly pure sound of a harp string being plucked is a connection to something deeply physical and almost beyond our understanding. You hear it, and something commands you to take a quick breath and take the sound within yourself. Whatever you were worrying about disappears, as you let yourself be absorbed completely by the music.

It's real therapy, and I highly recommend it. Get a harpist in your family, as I did.

I'm Walter Furley, and that is how I see it.

Boyhood Food

2 May 2008

I'm Walter Furley, and this is how I see it.

We like to watch the food channel at our house. We like the easy way those chefs put together fantastic meals, all within the time limits of the show, and sometimes we even get the recipes online and try them out. But the results are usually disappointing compared to what we saw on television.

And I'm beginning to wonder, does our food today really taste as good as the food we had when I was growing up back in the thirties?

I remember all the fresh vegetables from our garden, especially tomatoes, so red ripe and juicy with a real tomato taste. Sweet carrots we had to pull out of the muddy ground and wash off carefully before we took them to the kitchen. English peas, Kentucky Wonder beans, potatoes, beets, Boston lettuce, all sorts squash—all growing in a garden we tended every day. And in the summer, the fresh peaches and plums and pears and blackberries.

Maybe the favorite summer fruit was watermelon taken from the field, burst open, and then only the heart was eaten, because it had no seeds. Sunday nights after church, the whole congregation gathered outside for iced down watermelons or cantaloupes, a great reward for going to church.

And there were the great bakery treats Mom would make. Biscuits were fresh every morning, light and fluffy with fresh thick cream from our Jersey cow. And the leftovers were made into biscuit pudding with raisins and cinnamon and sometimes pecans baked with a heavy dose of cream. And breakfast usually included fried ham slices with eggs fried in the resulting grease, pancakes with molasses or honey we had taken from wild hives we found in the pasture there in Central Texas. All so good! Now Mom cooked with lard. It was in the biscuits, the pie crusts, fried chicken, beef cutlets, and likely many things of which I was not aware. And pure butter was used to flavor everything. Maybe that's why everything tasted so good.

Not today. Maybe that's why food today is disappointing to my palate. Those rich foods must have caused high cholesterol then, if they cause them today. How did we all survive? I feel today when I buy a watermelon and bite into that red juicy center, it's not the same. I have bought only a memory. But it is a lovely memory, and I am grateful to have it.

I'm Walter Furley, and that is how I see it.

Growing Up

2 May 2008

I'm Walter Furley, and this is the way I see it.

You know, when you reach your three score years and ten, you remember quite fondly your early childhood. Even though you have enjoyed a fine family of your own and seen your own children through their childhood, it's your own you recall and remember how you were so passionate about everything—games you played, what you ate, people you loved.

Growing up in Central Texas in the thirties meant you grew up in the Great Depression. While my family never had much money, I remember a very rich life in Marble Falls, Texas in those turbulent thirties. Everything was an adventure. A new school year meant a new teacher, some new friends, new books, and most of all, some new school clothes especially ordered from the Sears Roebuck Catalogue.

And they were definitely school clothes: a neatly ironed pair of khaki pants, a woven short-sleeved shirt, and a pair of tennis shoes during the warm months, an added jacket or sweater for the colder ones, and heavy leather shoes which were always a size too small because our feet had outgrown them by the time they arrived in the mail. But those school clothes came off the moment we came home because they had to last all year. So mama checked them for any needed washing so they would be ready for the next day. I remember having to be very careful at recess to keep the clothes clean.

But once home from school, we changed to short pants in the summer and went barefooted to do our chores and to play. The chores included herding in our two Jersey cows from the neighbor's pasture, milking the cows which meant once before school and again at night, chopping firewood for our kitchen stove, and more wood for the fireplace in winter. Playtime came after supper when children from the neighborhood gathered in the gravel covered streets to play games like red rover or Simon says or may I, or just running and chasing each other in games of tag.

The boys in the family slept on a screened-in sleeping porch, and we often listened with some apprehension to the night sounds of crickets or night birds and imagined great beasts nearby whenever the dogs barked loudly. There were small dogs and cats that we often slipped into bed with us, especially in cold weather with us all keeping snug under a pile of quilts, most of which were made by the women in the family.

Every day was an adventure—a cousin coming to visit, the high school football games, maybe going hunting for squirrels with Papa, a trip to town for maybe a frosted root beer at Michel's Drug Store, the first tomatoes in the garden, a chicken hawk threatening our chickens, new kittens and puppies being born.

One afternoon while herding in our cows, I found one had given birth to a calf. The little thing was still wet and breathing laboriously. I would have stayed to watch more, but the mother cow looked as if she was about to charge me, so I ran.

Those jokes about Saturday night baths were true then. The only water we had in the house was from a cistern that collected rain water, and when it was scarce, water was trucked home in barrels from the nearby creek. So daily baths were a wash-down from a basin and a well used washrag with special attention to dirty feet. Saturday was for tub baths. I wonder now how we survived without deodorant!

Were we living like that today, we would be considered below the poverty level. But we never knew that then. We were living a good life. And today I realize it was even better than we knew.

I'm Walter Furley, and that's the way I see it.

Chew You

13 May 2008

I'm Walter Furley, and this is how I see it.

I had a very interesting conversation with a lady in a restaurant the other day. Her table was next to mine, and she was gracious enough to tell me she listened to my editorials on KEDT and enjoyed them.

She said she is Hispanic and particularly likes the thoughts I expressed on our lazy use of language. She remembered in grade school learning the sounds for the letters of the alphabet and was thoroughly confused at the way students and some teachers sounded the letter "Y." Instead of saying "you" they said "chew," as in "don-chew like ice cream?" Or "don-chew do that?"

And the more I thought about it, I realized we do that all the time.

It's the juxtaposition of the "t" and the "y" that encourages the chew sound. Instead of "Don't you like ice cream" or "Don't you do that."

We say "doncha," which has no meaning at all.

I've already expressed my disdain for those who reduce the word "PRAH-bob-lee" to "PRAH-lee" and "NEW-que-lər" for "NEW-klee-ər" and other very careless pronunciations. But I realized I was quite guilty of "doncha."

It's embarrassing.

I know some Spanish, but when I hear it spoken on the streets, I suspect the reason I don't understand is because we tend to slur together syllables that should be distinctly separated. I was watching a French film recently, and thought my high school French should help me recognize some words, but even the French like to run syllables together. All of which is just fine if you are fluent in the language and accept the vocal shortcuts that everyone makes. But we who are trying to understand are trying to hear the words as we have learned to write them.

In my church choir, our director is always admonishing us singers to separate the "t" from "y" when we sing, "Cancha hear the angels singing" instead of "Can't you hear the angels singing." So even in church, we mispronounce.

All it takes is attention to detail, an effort to speak correctly, to make sure you are understood by everyone. Doncha know?

I'm Walter Furley and that's how I see it.

Grad Speaker

24 May 2008

I'm Walter Furley, and this is how I see it.

This is the time of year when students are graduated from high school and college, a time when they hear eminent speakers assure them they can be anything they choose to be, that the whole world is waiting for them out there.

I have never been asked to speak to a graduating class, likely for good reason, but if I were, I suspect I would tell them just what you would tell them. Be careful.

Achieving a diploma gives a student the right to feel self-confident, even superior. And with such an attitude, they often feel invulnerable, invincible, going to live forever, all that. They face dangers confidently, feeling safe in sampling the sins of the world.

We can tell them those sins are not all that great—some can kill you, all will diminish your life in one way or another, and if the kids would only ask us, who have been through those confident years, the times of straying are just not worth it. Learning to be sadder but wiser can cost a lot.

That's the negative side, the "don't" side.

The good side, the "do" side contains every mother's or father's advice and is usually dismissed as old-fashioned, not of today's world. But here's what we elders can say to any graduating class:

Always do the right thing, and that means always considering the consequences, especially to others. We are not alone; we are all connected.

Breaking little rules leads to breaking the big rules, and that means hurting others, hurting the environment, hurting yourself. And no courtroom can make a wrong a right.

So all you graduates who will listen to us elders, be careful. And remember, we have learned it's best to do the right thing.

I'm Walter Furley, and that's the way I see it.

Castor Oil

26 May 2008

I'm Walter Furley, and this is how I see it.

I recently overcame a minor, but long-lasting, bronchial condition that refused to respond to any medications prescribed by my doctor. Finally, both he and I decided I would just have to let it wear itself out.

It made me recall the time I was growing up in Marble Falls, Texas, when childhood afflictions struck. My mother was armed with an arsenal of medications like Vicks salve and mentholatum for colds, flax seed poultices for boils and skin problems, a terrible purple liquid called Gentian Violet for ring worm, kerosene for cleansing wounds caused by stepping on rusty nails, calamine lotion for sunburns, a drug store tonic called Baby Percy for stomach aches, Watkins Liniment for sore muscles, and many more which I have forgotten.

But one I remember quite vividly was castor oil. I remember the huge hideous glass bottle filled with the sickly yellow stuff, and the truly nauseating odor even when the cap was on the bottle. This was the medicine for everything, constipation, flu, anything that kept us from wanting to run and play. But administering the castor oil was no easy task. There was no way we children could open our mouth, take a spoonful, and go on our way. We fought with the ferocity of wild animals. I remember Mother saying it took three adults to hold me down to force me to swallow the castor oil. She had tried to hide it in a glass of orange juice, but there was no fooling anyone with that. The heavy oily odor could not be overcome with mere orange juice. To this day I cannot drink orange juice without remembering the taste of the castor oil, and always sniff to be sure the juice is pure. To be fair, I have to admit that the castor oil worked. Whatever was in my skinny little body causing trouble was gone within hours. So far as I know, castor oil is not prescribed today. And with good reason.

I have since learned that castor oil comes from the castor bean, which is also the source of the poison gas called ricin, which is now used by terrorists. But my dear family thought it was the best thing for whatever ailed me. And perhaps they were right. Here I am today, reasonably healthy, and hardly the worse for wear. But I'd still rather be sick than take castor oil.

I'm Walter Furley, and that's how I see it.

Gas Tanks

5 June 2008

I'm Walter Furley, and this is how I see it.

Does it ever seem to you that the business world is just out to annoy us just for their own sadistic pleasure? Well it does to me.

Take gas tanks for instance. Why aren't they all on the same side of the car? My wife's car has the gas tank on the right, on the passenger's side. We have to be sure we drive up to the pump with that side next to it. My car has the gas tank on the left side, the driver's side, and somehow it's easier to maneuver the car up to the pump properly that way. But if you drive more than one model, it's a real effort to remember on which side the gas tank is located. And when you park with the pump on the wrong side, prepare for some high blood pressure and loud complaints. If only the manufacturers would hold a summit, all get together, and agree to put the gas tank opening on the driver's side, no exceptions. It would do just that much more to make life easier.

And while I am talking of gas pumps, why aren't gas prices uniform?

There's little, apparently, we can do about high prices, but why aren't they all the same? Today we needed a fill up and heard of a station across town with gas six cents cheaper a gallon. We drove through slow traffic (goodness knows how much gas we used) to get there, and sure enough it was cheaper. And sure enough there was a waiting line a block long to get to the pumps. So we had to drive back to our neighborhood station, fill up at the higher price, and grit our teeth at the futility of it all. If you dealers are going to raise the prices, raise them all, and don't tease us with a single station that drops the price just enough to make us drive five miles to save fifty cents. That is just as aggravating as the high prices themselves.

I'm Walter Furley and that is how I see it.

Sump'n'

5 June 2008

I'm Walter Furley and this us how I see it.

I should like to enlist every one of you in the systematic elimination of a word—it's not even a word—a sound from our English language. That nonsense sound is SUMP-n as in "sump'n' smells bad," or "get sump'n' at the store," or "there's sump'n' out there."

How much effort does it take to say the word "something"? None.

Yet, I hear television newscasters say "sump'n's going on in Washington."

Or weather casters saying "sump'n's brewing in the Gulf."

Imagine you are just learning English, and you get all the words learned correctly, then hear someone say "there's sump'n' wrong."

How can we explain it. I am alarmed by the practice because I find myself using it often. It just comes out without my thinking. And I know it's true of you and everyone else.

We could do ourselves, our language, our entire civilization a great benefit if we really worked to eliminate the embarrassing sound from our collective heads. Say, "something." Something. If we could do that, it would really be—something.

I'm Walter Furley, and that's how I see it.

Tattoo

18 June 2008

I'm Walter Furley, and this is how I see it.

I truly do not understand tattooing. Why do perfectly good-looking people have something burned into their skin to mar their bodies for life?

I have several friends who were in Nazi concentration camps and were forced to have a serial numbers burned into their arms by insidious prison guards. These victims don't display the numbers but will willing show them to you to help you believe just how inhumane the Nazis were to fellow human beings.

A beautiful young lady worked in my studio a few years ago. She was not only beautiful, but very efficient, affable, dependable, everything a good employee should be. But one day she wore sandals to work, and I noticed a pink rose tattooed on her ankle with a wreath of leaves encircling the entire ankle. The tattoo was very pretty, decorative, and I suppose tastefully placed. But why? I never asked her of course and never even mentioned I had noticed it. But the question remained.

Since then I have noticed other such markings displayed on bare body parts. At a wedding a bride in an exquisite gown was marched down the aisle, and when she arrived at the alter, we all could see a lovely butterfly tattooed on her lower back. It was an almost backless gown.

Those instances, I must admit are tasteful and even attractive, but because of the natural beauty of the ladies, so unnecessary.

Then you take the tattoos so many men wear. Designs are covering their entire arms with special emphasis on a tiger, or lion, and even a snake on the bulging biceps. Other guys proudly walk along the seawall or beach wearing only shorts to show off tattoos over their entire visible body, including their legs, neck, and in some cases their faces. As a child I was appalled and fascinated to go to the circus to see the tattooed people and paid a quarter to see them. I wonder if those people can get jobs anymore with all the competition out on the street.

It's my personal philosophy that you prepare yourself to go out in public looking as least objectionable as possible—neat, clean, that sort of thing. To wear something that would actually call attention to yourself is rude and even offensive, except in the case of ladies, of course, with their makeup and hats and low-cut dresses. Men were there to see, but not to be seen.

I hope those who wear tattoos are happy with them. The tattoos are there for life. I do notice, however, in the television news clips that many of those arrested for one thing or another have many tattoos. And again, I ask, "Why?"

I'm Walter Furley, and that's the way I see it.

Grandmother's Dresses

24 June 2008

I'm Walter Furley, and this is how I see it.

The recent news stories about the polygamous compound in West Texas showed the women wearing dresses much like those my grandmother wore when I was a child. The high neckline, the sleeves down to the wrist, and a hem line just above the ankles fit the pattern of every dress I ever saw my dear grandmother wear. She was well into her seventies when I was a child, but I remember the same style dress for every occasion. I never saw her do it, but she told how she had pulled the plow while grandfather guided it to make furrows in the large garden they cultivated for the family's vegetables. She did it in a long-sleeved dress. I did see her chopping firewood for the wood cook stove in a similar dress. It was just the way she dressed for all occasions. Sunday brought out her black dress and hat, but the long sleeves and hem remained the same. And she always looked regal. Whether the dress was checked gingham or a heavier material for the Sunday dress, she stood straight and tall as she could, always smiling and often laughing with us children.

So the dresses worn by the women in the news stories about the polygamy case evoked a warm nostalgia for me. And I couldn't help but wonder, were those women like my grandmother? Her dress reflected her modesty. She was very religious, and we would walk a full mile each Sunday with her to get to Sunday school and church.

Is this dress style on these women a reflection of such modesty and piety also? I don't know what their philosophy is and if it is reflected in their clothing style. But that style recalled to me a grandmother who was a lady, who lived a life of real labor in maintaining her house and family, and who did it with great love and happiness. I can only hope those women in their long dresses are enjoying the same.

I'm Walter Furley, and that's how I see it.

Opera Singers

1 August 2008

I'm Walter Furley, and this is how I see it.

The Olympic athletes are in the news constantly these days, and we all watch in wonder at their amazing feats.

But I recently watched some performers accomplish amazing feats which will never be part of the Olympics.

It was at the opera.

This summer my wife and I indulged ourselves and attended the opera in Santa Fe, New Mexico, a truly enchanting place and an amazing opera house. It is built in a Depression by a mountain canyon with modern facilities and staging but in the open air. Had it rained during the performance we would have been soaked. Even so, the place was packed because the Santa Fe Opera has a reputation for excellence and perfect acoustics. And it lived up to that reputation for our visit. The opera was one by Handel, called *Radomisto* and tells an archaic tale of kings conquering countries, and taking queens and princesses as new members of a harem—very convoluted, and frankly, very hard to follow.

But the singing! There were only six characters in the opera and each had long solos with impossible singing lines that required as much energy as any Olympic athlete. And the music was simply beautiful, and the singers sang exquisitely, tossing off twenty-minute arias with apparent ease with captivating beauty. The physical effort of singing that long and that loud and that beautifully required years of preparation, years of practice, to say nothing of astounding talent.

One of the characters was a counter tenor, a man who could sing in the soprano range. He was, for lack of a better word, unbelievable. And you know these singers have to watch every aspect of their life, their health, their diet to be sure their voices stay in shape, to be sure they can deliver the music at the moment it is called for, just as athletes do—train, practice, keep in shape. But singers have to be sure it is done beautifully and artistically as well perfectly and powerfully.

I think that puts opera singers in a class higher than athletes.

I'm Walter Furley, and that is how I see it.

M. Givens

3 August 2008

I'm Walter Furley, and this is how I see it.

I truly enjoy Murphy Givens' columns in the *Caller-Times*, and his spots here on KEDT-FM. He seems to have an inexhaustible resource for local history and takes these moments and events of the distant past and makes them alive and current today.

I can't drive down Staples Street or pass Ropes Park or the many other city streets without wondering about the men for whom they were named. Most of the events and people he writes about were here over a hundred years ago. It's fascinating to imagine the large homes on the Bluff overlooking the bay and the businesses and boarding houses down below teeming with activity and right next to the water on Water Street. And it's hard to imagine Ocean Drive as a dirt or shell road as a pathway for horses and wagons.

In years before the city was built, the Bluff and Ocean Drive were fine points for the Karancahua Indians to stand and look out, testing the weather or looking for fishing activity. And what about Padre Island with the many shipwrecks in the sixteen hundreds, ships loaded with treasure or with supplies for explorers to land and claim the coast for their home country. I recall the story of one wreck loaded with families coming here to colonize the land having to wander up and down the burning sands of Padre, only to be attacked by the resident Indians and slaughtered on the dunes. What artifacts lie buried in the sand there—jewelry the women might have hidden, tools and utensils that might have salvaged from the wreck hoping to make a home here in spite of the shipwreck. Even today we hear of Spanish coins washing up on the beaches of Padre.

Murphy Givens makes every inch of our coast a goldmine of history.

Where we may see a nice lot for a new home or a spot on the island for a picnic, there have been thousands of people who have been to that very spot before spending a part of their lifetime, just as we are now. Murphy reminds us our city is the sum of all who have come before: the Indians, the Spanish, the French, the Irish, people from all parts of the world adding their part of history to make the area what it is today.

I'm Walter Furley, and that's the way I see it.

Migraine

3 Aug 2008

I'm Walter Furley, and this is how I see it.

A few years ago, I was prone to suffer migraine headaches so severe they demanded bed rest.

On a visit to a friend's house, I was attacked by a severe migraine and asked for a spot in which to lie down. She happened to be a practicing psychologist, and said she could cure that headache.

She told me to lie on the bed, to stay as calm and still as possible.

Then to breathe in slowly counting to eight, hold the breath for a count of eight, then release the breath slowly counting to eight.

Well it took all my concentration to keep breathing slowly while counting, more control to hold the breath while counting, and even more to release it slowly while counting to eight. That was all I could think of while doing the exercise. It was occupying all my thoughts, all my energy, until I could no longer think about my migraine.

After doing exercise just a few times, I actually went to sleep, and when I awoke after about a quarter hour, I felt wonderful—relaxed, refreshed, and most of all, headache free.

I've found the exercise useful in other ways. When I get tense or frustrated over some chore, if I stop and do the exercise, I get control of myself and can continue my mission. I even use the exercise to get to sleep. If others are watching television or on the telephone, I can escape to the world of sleep with no bother whatsoever.

I share this with you because I have come to the conclusion that we bring on our own headaches and migraines and likely other physical ailments by concentrating on them, letting the negative control us.

My friend's simple breathing exercise seems to purge me of any tension or worry and releases my mind and perhaps my body to do that which I really want it to do. It gives me back control.

I think it would do the same for anyone. So I want to share it with you. Here's the prescription: Breathe in slowly for a count of eight, hold it for a count of eight, breathe out for a count of eight. Repeat as needed.

I'm Walter Furley, and that's the way I see it.

Millionaire Homes

19 August 2008

I'm Walter Furley, and this is how I see it.

I recently came across a catalogue of the Christie's Auction House, the one that auctions famous art works for millions of dollars. It also auctions or sells fabulous estates all over the world. The catalogue has beautiful glossy pictures of hundreds of enormous homes, best described as castles, with many, many rooms, acres of grounds, and perfect landscaping. Of course, they cost millions. Some, just one or two, but many marked at multi-million dollar price tags.

It's wonderful to look at them all, great halls and rooms truly fit for a king, each with enchanting views of mountains or the sea or really amazing gardens, swimming pools, horse barns, everything.

But I was immediately struck by how many were for sale. The catalogue has over 200 pages, and each one has a very expensive house described on it, many as big as hotels, all waiting for the right buyer. One is priced at 47 million dollars.

I wonder what the down payment would be, and what would be the monthly payments, and what would be the taxes, and what would it cost to run a forty-seven million dollar house. What housewife would want to dust and polish a 40 room mansion with spiral staircases and hundreds of window panes? There would have to be servants, many servants, who would want a pretty good salary each. Why that 47 million is just the tip of the iceberg.

Many of these homes are in Connecticut. Some in Colorado, the Virgin Islands, Mexico, South America, but there are several in Houston and Dallas. There seem to be millionaires everywhere wanting to get rid of their homes.

Is the crisis in the housing market affecting them, too? Are there some who can no longer make the payments on the 45 million dollar loan? I suspect people who bought such property paid cash up front and expect to get cash in return when they sell it. So obviously loan money is of no concern to them, as it is to us who must be happy with a home in Nueces County appraised far below 47 million.

Beautiful as these estates are, I wonder if they know happy families living there. With as many as 15 bedrooms, there must have been children. If so, why don't the families keep the homes for their children to live in, raising their own families, instead of selling them.

I'm sure each mansion has a story, not all of them happy. Planning and building the homes took not only a lot of money but a lot of imagination, talent, and work, only to be eventually sold by Christie's auction house.

I won't be bidding on them. I am content just to look at the hundreds of pictures of magnificent mansions, all for sale.

I'm Walter Furley, and that is how I see it.

Mispronouncing

19 August 2008

I'm Walter Furley, and this is how I see it.

I'm always surprised and a little amazed when I get mail regarding these little commentaries on KEDT-FM. I think of them as amusing, not thought provoking.

But a recent one on our local mispronunciations provoked a very good letter from Kip Foss in Ingleside. He too grinds his teeth when people say "prolly" for probably, and adds these little butcheries to the list.

Why do we drop the double letter *l* so often, as in "WI-yum" for *William*, or "BI-yun" for billion. Or even the single letter *l*, as in "VA-yoo" for *value*? And how often have you heard "KAB-i-dal" for *capital*.

Or "SUP-pos-ablee" for *supposedly*? Or "TET-na-kal" for *technical*.

And even people from Pennsylvania call it "Pen-sa-VAYN-yah" ignoring the L sound.

And then Kip Foss really gets going. Listen to this: "What can be done with the people, especially adults who should know better, who can't say more than three words in a row without injecting *like* in the sentence? Or those girls, and they are almost all girls, who still talk like the Valley Girls from the 1990s. They have that odd lilt in the voices with that little up-turned question. It's like they don't know."

And Kip Foss taught me something I really didn't know. It's wrong to say "kil-LAHM-e-ter." The word is a measurement in meters, so it is a KIL-o-met-er. It designates a thousand meters. The *ometer* segment designates an instrument, such as speedometer, thermometer, barometer. I must have slept through that session of general science class.

So, thank you Kip Foss for a great letter. I liked it not only because you agree with me, you taught me something.

I'm Walter Furley, and that is how I see it.

New Bayfront Plans

13 October 2008

I'm Walter Furley, and this is how I see it.

The city is asking us citizens to submit our ideas and plans for the further development of the Corpus Christi Bayfront.

I've voiced my ideas previously, but since no one has rushed to support them, I feel obligated to voice them again.

I can visualize a whole grove of myrtle trees along the Bayfront, mixed in with the palm trees there now, with the massive pink blossoms standing up like huge strawberry ice cream cones. The myrtles seem to bloom all summer long, and with a long display of them along the Bayfront, it would give the same beautiful impression that the cherry blossoms give to Washington in the spring. The trees are still attractive in the winter, and could be enhanced with flower beds around each tree, such as you see in London and Paris.

Also, I have a vision of a gigantic sundial on the Bayfront. With all our sunny days it would always be working. The gnomon should be very tall, about twenty feet, casting a shadow on a tile floor where the hours would be marked in a colorful and artistic style. There could be benches with shades above them around the gnomon, perhaps with a fountain or two, making it a real centerpiece of the Bayfront, helping give the city an unforgettable and unique personality. I have seen pictures of such sundials and parks in European cities, and they are real landmarks for tourists and visitors. The styles are varied from stark modern designs to florid antique creations, but all perfectly aligned with the longitude to give a correct reading of the time of day.

I've no idea how much such a creation would cost, or how we would agree on a design to please everyone. But I find it an exciting idea, and wish everyone did.

I'm Walter Furley, and that's way I see it.

Hurricane Ike

14 September 2008

I'm Walter Furley, and this is how I see it.

The videos of the damage in Galveston and Houston caused by Hurricane Ike looked hauntingly familiar, like the damage we knew from hurricane Celia in 1970. The piles of wreckage, so extensive you wonder how it will ever be cleaned up, the mounds of glass in the streets from broken windows in the high rise office buildings, the huge trees uprooted and covering the streets, the flooding that is keeping people from getting back in their homes, all had been experienced before by us in Corpus Christi thirty-eight years ago.

I remember seeing people sitting on their lawns in Pharaoh Valley with their fine brick homes leveled behind them, one with a sign reading "For Sale Cheap." The Driscoll Hotel looked like something in a ghost town, widows broken, curtains and blinds blowing in the wind. Boats in the marina were capsized or blown into each other, many damaged beyond repair. And various parts of town were heavily damaged, while others were almost untouched. And the trees, which we need, so badly broken and lying across streets completely blocking any traffic. One television tower was blown down, and my own station, KZTV, was so badly damaged it was off the air for more than two weeks. But then, power was out over much of the city, so there were few that could watch TV.

I remember the heat wave that followed, hot humid air, with no wind to cool us, and certainly no power to run air conditioners. Misery was rampant.

But we who survived Celia can tell those who survived Ike that everything eventually gets put back to normal. Chain saws cut up the trees and clear the streets. Telephone and power workers eventually get to your house and put everything back in order. Homes are rebuilt, often better than before. And while the time right after the storm was so overwhelming, as the days go by the world seems to right itself.

And, as in Celia, there was almost no loss of life in Hurricane Ike. We who remained stood in the wreckage and called ourselves lucky. Galveston and Houston will do the same.

The job ahead is daunting, but it will get done, just as it always has. Remember, Galveston survived the worst hurricane in history back in 1900 when 6000 people were lost. Ike was just a wanna-be compared to that one. Everything's going to be all right.

I'm Walter Furley, and that's the way I see it.

M. Truman

September 15, 2008

I'm Walter Furley, and this is how I see it.

I was saddened to learn of the death of Margaret Truman earlier this year. The daughter of one of our country's greatest presidents had made a career for herself in radio and as the author of a best selling series of mystery novels all set in Washington, DC.

I had worked with her in New York in the late fifties when I was an assistant producer of the NBC radio show called "Weekday." It starred Margaret Truman and Mike Wallace and was broadcast each weekday from 10:00 AM to 4:00 PM. It was a wonderful show created by a fellow Corpus Christi native Allen Ludden, who later became most famous for the TV game show "Password."

"Weekday" featured a musical guest each day with their recordings played throughout the show, interviews with almost every celebrity who happened to be in New York that day, serial versions of best selling novels, ten-minute lectures by such people as historian Bruce Catton, actress Helen Hayes, anthropologist Margaret Mead, baby-raising advice by Dr. Spock—so many, I can't remember them all.

But I do remember Margaret. She came to the studio each morning looking lovely and smiling, partly because the studio had a huge picture window through which tourists could watch the show, but mostly because Margaret Truman was a classy lady and felt she had to always give a fine impression as a president's daughter. Because the show was live, we often featured political people involved in the day's news. And Margaret had a very good memory of some of those people.

If they had ever crossed her father or maligned him, she refused to stay in the studio for the interview. Mike Wallace had to do the job. On the other hand, she insisted in doing solo interviews with friends of her father like Eleanor Roosevelt or politicians who were Democrats.

She also could get very angry. When she learned that Mike Wallace was being paid much more than she, the NBC brass knew about it right away. Margaret never missed a show to my memory, but she was very sharp with some of the producers and broadcast executives, and she got a raise to equal Mike's pay. The show closed after a year, when radio networks lost their affiliates who chose to be independent and make more money playing records and reading commercials.

That era was the end of radio soap operas, game shows, and all network program production with the exception of newscasts.

But you notice there are no NBC, CBS, or ABC radio stations anymore. Margaret Truman won many fans with her radio show "Weekday." She won several broadcasting awards for her work there. My duty each day was to stand by the control board, monitoring the script, and ready to get anything Margaret needed as the show progressed. She was a great lady, and I, as a broadcaster just out of college, adored her.

I'm Walter Furley, and that's how I see it.

Greed

26 September 2008

I'm Walter Furley, and this is how I see it.

The country's economic crisis has reached almost unbelievable proportions.

Some banks lent too much money to people who now cannot pay it back, and now those banks don't have enough money left to stay in business. And not just small banks, the biggest in the nation.

Economics experts say the banks encouraged borrowers to take big loans without finding out if they could pay them back. These loans were then bundled together and sold to other banks who sold them to other banks, until billions of dollars were tied up in loans which no one could pay. The scheme was supposed to pay off in billions to the banks holding the loans.

The sole motivation seems to have been greed—not entirely with the banks, but with the people asking for the loans.

Figures show most of the loans were on new houses. Instead of building a modest frame or brick veneer dwelling, too many borrowers wanted dream homes, castles with multiple bedrooms and enormous bathrooms, landscaped estates. Contractors and builders greedily signed on to build such houses, most of which must surely have been obviously out of the means of the homeowners.

Instead of telling the home buyers they should allocate only a percentage of their income toward the house, analysts say the banks encouraged them to overbuild and failed to even ascertain how the loan could be paid for. The bank was going to sell the loan anyway.

Millionaire athletes and movie stars and perhaps some oilmen could afford to over build and overspend, though many of them went into financial troubles in this crisis.

But we ordinary people should have had better sense. We were perhaps mesmerized by the fact that homes for which we once paid twenty-thousand dollars are now appraised at over a hundred thousand dollars. And the prices just got bigger each year. We should have known that such an increase in value had to have a limit, even with inflation. Well, it obviously did have a limit, and what the outcome will be is yet to be determined.

The motto of "living within your means" is still a good one and may become one that is enforced by strong painful reality.

It isn't nice to be greedy. It isn't safe either. Just remember: greed can start with any of us. But greed starts growing like an infection, and before you know it, we are where we are today.

I'm Walter Furley, and that is how I see it.

Pavarotti

26 September 2008

I'm Walter Furley, and this is how I see it.

I saw a wonderful PBS special celebrating the famous tenor, Luciano Pavarotti. He had one of the most exciting voices in history, perhaps better than Caruso. His death this year marked a real loss in our opera history.

There are those who say he sang too long, that he should have retired a few years ago when he was still in his prime. Other singers have retired at the peak of the careers—Beverly Sills, Joan Sutherland, Benamino Gigli. But Pavarotti loved to sing, and as long as people would pay to hear him, he would sing. I don't know who persuaded him to be a part of the trio known as "The Three Tenors" along with Domingo and Carreras, but they found it to be a gold mine and performed their trio concerts for several years and sold millions of recordings. But even then, the critics said Pavarotti was not as glittering as he once was. Even when he died, he had booked concerts right up until the last minute, when he had to cancel them and be hospitalized.

I can certainly understand Pavarotti's wish to keep singing. Like all opera singers, he had to be blessed with a beautiful voice, he had to pay expensive teachers to train him, and he had to practice and keep in shape every day of his life. Singing was his life. To give up singing would be to give up living. And his reputation in music history likely will not suffer. He was that great.

There is something grievous about such artists when they reach that point where they can no longer be the great performers they once were. To have gone through all that training, and no longer be able to use it. But we know and they know that moment always comes.

Pavarotti delayed the inevitable as long as he could. And even if his voice was fading, he went out with a glory that few of us can even dream of.

I'm Walter Furley, and that's how I see it.

Election

6 November 2008

I'm Walter Furley, and this is how I see it.

I am relieved that the election is over. I admit my candidate did not win even though I thought him the most seasoned and reasonable man to run the country. But I can live with the people's choice and admit I find a lot to admire in him.

But we must all remember that it was a very close election—50 million for Obama, 46 million for McCain. The majority is over by less than four percent. So the winner must face the fact that 46 million did not want him for their leader. Where he leads must be in a path we will follow. I don't think that is going to be too difficult.

His problems are already our problems: our money and our safety.

Both are endangered at the moment, and whether he can bring them under control or not, we must all work together to try.

If we don't work together, neither will be solved.

I was reading this week how Andrew Jackson had to threaten to go to war against radicals in South Carolina who disagreed with him so strongly the state wanted to secede. Abraham Lincoln had to go to war to keep the country united, knowing that if any state seceded the great American nation would disintegrate. The painful result left the nation ravaged by the conflict, but the Union still united.

Today we see the wisdom of that effort. It has been together that we have survived the conflicts that have followed, and it will be together that we survive any in the future.

So, whose side are we on? We are on the side of our country, whoever is leading it. We are no longer a part of the 51 percent or the 48 percent; we are part of the 100 percent—100 percent American.

I'm Walter Furley, and that's how I see it.

Red Light Ticket

20 November 2008

I'm Walter Furley, and this is how I see it.

I have a confession to make: I committed a crime.

I know, I never thought I would do it either, but the proof is there.

I received in the mail an official looking envelope from the city traffic department saying I was photographed running a red light, and there was a picture of my car with a closeup picture of my license plate.

There was no doubt about it. My car, all alone at the intersection of Doddridge and Ocean Drive.

And there was seventy-five dollar fine due in a few weeks. I am still thoroughly shaken.

But in my defense, my access to downtown is Ocean Drive. And my access to Ocean drive is Doddridge Street, and Doddridge Street has been torn up for several months, requiring me to take neighborhood streets as a detour to Ocean Drive.

At the time, Doddridge Street was completely closed to Ocean Drive, so in my opinion that was no need for a light there at all. No traffic could enter or leave from Doddridge, so why should traffic be stopped there.

Yet, the traffic lights were still functioning and so was that blasted camera. I think I have a real case against the traffic department, but a lawyer would cost much more than the seventy-five dollars, so I can only pay the fine. I wonder if I could pay it to some worthy cause instead of the traffic court, say KEDT. I might even get one of those premium prizes. But the city needs my seventy-five dollars, I'm sure to fix potholes, if nothing else.

Now I certainly believe in safe driving and certainly believe red-light drivers should be caught and punished. But I am devastated to realize I am one of them.

So, I come to you today in deep contrition to inform you: those red light cameras do work. Very well.

I'm Walter Furley and that is how I see it.

Electronic Toys

10 December 2008

I'm Walter Furley, and this is how I see it.

This Thanksgiving as the family got together, a young relative showed off his newest gift to himself, a new telephone that was a computer and television all included.

I couldn't believe it. It was about the size of the palm of his hand, with a screen maybe two by three inches in size, with a seemingly unlimited menu of things the telephone could do. Touch one section and a keyboard appears. You can type a message right there on the little screen, find a telephone number, and send the message to someone who had the same phone.

Touch another part of the little screen, and you get a map showing where various restaurants are nearby. And it had his entire telephone directory recorded, so when he scrolled down to the name he wanted, the thing automatically dialed the number.

It could download music and store a whole repertoire of hit records to be played back into little ear pods that sounded like my hi fidelity LPs. It could play video games.

Oh, there was so much more that little sliver of a box could do. I didn't understand all it did, much less how to make it do it. It would take a college course to learn how to operate it. It could even connect to the Internet, though I can't see the value of reading it on a two inch screen when I have trouble reading my seventeen inch computer screen. The outfit is ostensibly a telephone, and you can actually dial (if that's the word) up any number, and I must say the reception was quite clear and loud.

Ah, but the most astounding thing was it was also a camera. The young man could take a picture, then transmit it to someone else's telephone or computer anywhere in the country, maybe the world.

And just to make it all too much, he could download movies, complete movies, and watch them there on the little two by three inch screen.

I just spent nearly two thousand dollars for a 46-inch HDTV. I am not about to start watching TV on a two-inch screen.

I don't know. The world is moving so fast lately, and things like this telephone are just too, too complicated.

I think the whole world was better off with the big black dial telephones. So much easier to use, and they weren't there in our pocket to ring obscenely and disturb your time away from the—well, from the telephone.

I'm Walter Furley, and that's the way I see it.

The Night Before Christmas

10 December 2008

I'm Walter Furley, and this is how I see it.

Our Christmas traditions are just barely old enough to be called traditions. The Christmas tree was brought over by German immigrants in the 1700s, Santa Claus by the Dutch around 1800, and we Americans just kept adding to the Christmas legend. Then in 1823, Clement Clark Moore wrote a poem for his children's Christmas that put Santa in a sleigh, with eight reindeer, and sliding down a chimney with toys. But it was the words of the poem that created the vision of Santa in our imagination.

The famous newspaper cartoonist, Thomas Nast, gave us perhaps the first picture of Santa when he drew him in a fur trimmed suit with a sack of toys, and showing his headquarters as the North Pole.

The cartoon was in black and white and drawn in 1860. Then in 1931 Coca Cola ads put Santa in color—a bright red suit, white fur trim, wavy white beard, and a red and white pointed cap. And the pictures elaborated on the North Pole toy headquarters with elves working endlessly to fill Santa's pack.

Then in 1939 an advertising writer for Montgomery Ward wrote a bit of doggerel about Rudolph the Red-nosed Reindeer, and Gene Autry had it set to music—and a best selling record. The Santa Claus legend had grown even more.

But it was Moore, Clement Clark Moore, who inspired all the others to contribute to the Santa story (and in spite of Rudolph, the Coca Cola Santa or the one drawn by Mr. Nast) created the most enduring and endearing picture. You've heard it already this year, but it bears listening to again.

I'm Walter Furley and that is how I see it.

Price Is Right

24 December 2008

I'm Walter Furley and this is how I see it.

When I was a TV news anchor, I never had time to watch daytime TV. Now that I have retired, I've discovered "The Price Is Right," and I think it is a wonderful show. It seems to be a microcosm of the American dream, or some dream, anyway. All those people from all walks of life striving and hoping for a chance to win some great prizes for free. You don't have to be especially smart, just aware of what most things cost and willing to let the rest of the world see you guess.

It's interesting, of not amazing, what people wear knowing they are going to be on national television. Most are in clothes suitable for working in the yard, T-shirt, shorts, almost no skirts or suits, except for those in the military. They always wear spic and span uniforms, likely because they know there's a better chance of being selected for the contest. And there's always a great surge of crowd support for them when they win and great sympathy when they fail.

But it is the interaction between myself and the show that makes it so exciting. I can't help but bid or guess on the prices of the items offered and often feel I have actually won when I am right. Even the spin off wheel gets me worked up. I grunt with great effort as they give it a spin and snort in disgust when they don't spin hard enough.

And when little old ladies need help getting the wheel to going, I grit my teeth and tense up to help them. Retirement means a lot of free time on your hands.

I have no plans on ever being a contestant on "The Price Is Right."

And frankly some of the prizes would be no prize at all to me, such as immense hot tubs, a roomful of exercise equipment, a year's supply of anything. I would like the all expense paid trips to anywhere, and I would like a new car. But so would the hundreds of people in each audience and millions across the nation who are watching along with me.

So it is quite enough to have that hour to relax after breakfast and the morning chores, and then plan where to go have lunch.

And there, as everywhere, we go where the price is right.

I'm Walter Furley, and that's how I see it.

2009

Weeds

24 January 2009

I'm Walter Furley, and this is how I see it.

I've been fighting weeds in our flower garden, and there is one in particular which will not be conquered.

I've never learned its name, but it grows in straight stalks usually about a foot high with little petals all up and down it that look like fat hairs. I once heard it referred to as mother-in-law's tongue, but that is too long a name and does not apply to the mothers-in-law I know. The weed is easily pulled up. The roots seem to grow mostly on the surface. But for every one I pull up, two or three seem to grow in its place. It's like an infection or bacteria.

Well, this past two weeks I have been under the weather and not at all interested in a flower garden. But one morning I strolled out and found that weed had grown a stem about four feet high and put forth a mass of blossoms that were absolutely beautiful, dozens of small bell-shaped blossoms all colored a bright coral. What's more, several more such weeds had done the same thing. This long stem with plump little gray-colored petals running all up and down, but now with a bare stem reaching up high with this full cluster of beautiful blossoms. They've been there a week now, and with the windy weather, still standing. And I couldn't help but think, "What if a large group of them were planted together, what a lovely sight they would make with the full head of beautiful coral-colored flowers." And they are just weeds. Imagine.

Of course, I was reminded of the ugly duckling story and the many others where the unattractive turns into a thing of beauty. And I recalled that in growing up I was regarded as a skinny, acne-afflicted teenager, last to be chosen for the team, having difficulty to find dates for the prom. A real weed of a boy. And look at me now. But, I don't think I have blossomed yet. And I'm wondering if I ever will. I marked my eightieth birthday this past year, which implies the warranty is running out.

But I'm still here. There's still hope. Some of us weeds sometime take a little longer to become beautiful.

So I'm taking a lesson from the weeds in my garden. Just wait. My best is yet to come.

I'm Walter Furley, and that is how I see it.

Inaugural Music
26 January 2009

I'm Walter Furley, and this is how I see it.

Weren't the inaugural ceremonies impressive last week?

The crowds were estimated to be in the millions, in spite of eighteen degree weather. I confess I would not have gone out in that weather or stood all that time in that crowd for anything. Though I appreciate those who did and say they did it just because they wanted to be a part of it. But standing many blocks away and watching the event on a television screen is not my idea or being a "part of it."

I admired all the participants, especially the two presidents and their first ladies who endured it all with great elegance. And the parade was a real stunner. All those hundreds of participants standing in line for hours before the parade even began are to my mind almost martyrs to the cause. But the really beautiful part of the ceremony was the special music played by Itzhak Perlman on the violin, Yo-Yo Ma on the cello, and other world-known musicians playing a clarinet and, of all things, a grand piano all out there in the frigid cold.

At the time I marveled at the flawless sound pickup. Each instrument perfectly balanced, no wind noise, and performers playing with smiles on their faces. An heroic performance, if ever there was one. Then we learned the music was prerecorded and the players were miming their parts. And that made perfect sense. I had worried that Perlman was exposing that million dollar Stradivarius he plays to below-freezing temperatures. And Yo-Yo Ma's cello is just as valuable. And that grand piano. How would they ever keep the instruments in tune with the extreme temperatures. Had they been performing live, their sound would have reached only those in the immediate vicinity. To be heard elsewhere, it had to be amplified, and if it is amplified, then it would be heard in the same process as a recording. It makes you wonder. However did anyone think such music could even be performed under such circumstances? And I am relieved to learn that the musicians did *not* use their priceless instruments, but some lesser ones borrowed for the occasion. Even so, it was a miracle that they could manipulate their fingers at all, much less make beautiful music. And it was beautiful. And it was gratifying to me to see classical music included in such a national and patriotic event. It made me feel included somehow.

I'm Walter Furley, and that is how I see it.

Wrist Watch Time

6 February 2009

I'm Walter Furley, and this is how I see it.

I'm a stickler for the correct time. This was born I suspect out the 45 years I spent in TV keeping newscasts on time. The station had to join the network at the precise top of the hour, so as we counted 56, 57, 58, 59, we pressed a button at 60 and put CBS on the air.

Since leaving the station, however, I have no access to that precise timing, so I on occasion revisit the studio just to re-set my watch.

That way, when I watch at home, I can once again count the seconds on my watch to see if the station still joins the network on time. For the record, it does. And I have the satisfaction of knowing that my wristwatch is keeping the exact time wherever I am.

However, I have a friend who boasts a satellite watch, which he says automatically shows the exact time. So I compared watches, and saw that his was three minutes slow. I condescendingly pointed out to him that my watch was set precisely to the TV network time. He more graciously pointed out that his was showing exact sun time, the exact time for Corpus Christi, Texas, while mine was showing Greenwich Mean Time, or the time used within the Central Time Zone and other time zones all over the world.

He of course was very smug about having the *real* correct time.

But if he wanted to watch the six o'clock news he would have to tune in three minutes early to hit it on time or miss the first few stories.

Also, if I make an appointment with him, I could be three minutes late and still get there on time.

Satellite time would never work in radio or television. Every time zone is set to the same seconds within the hour with the hours changing at the time zone borders. Perfectly logically and practical, even if the times are off within the zone borders. So enjoy your satellite time. My wristwatch tells me exactly when NPR goes on the air, and what's more important than that.

I'm Walter Furley, and that's the way I see it.

Respect

10 February 2009

I'm Walter Furley, and this is how I see it.

I think I have figured out what is wrong with our civilization today.

There is a great lack of respect.

I mean respect for just about everything.

The most obvious case is the way television comedians feel so free to make fun of our president. Granted they have good cause at times, but there seems to be no limit to what they can say about the person running our country. I at first thought it was a personal thing against president George W. Bush, but with the new president in office, the jokes and criticism are getting to be just as virulent.

But the lack of respect doesn't stop there. Congress members get barbs just as quickly, and these are the people making our laws, looking out for our country's welfare. There should be a way to question or dissent with those in public office without resorting to abject ridicule and insults.

I see lack of respect in letters to the editors in our newspaper. People who serve with little compensation but give untold hours of study and work to the community are subject to that same ridicule and attacks.

Our schools discipline problems are in every case the lack of respect shown teachers by some students. I can remember when teachers were next to saints in the community and were always shown honor and great respect—not the insults and even physical attacks we see reported today.

And I would even go so far as to say that today's divorce rate is because of a lack of respect among spouses. If you have love along with respect for your spouse, you could never be unfaithful and or cause hurt and abuse.

I wonder if we have been conditioned by TV comedy shows to make fun of our leaders. There is an undercurrent in much of our entertainment that demeans all our rules for being civil, for being polite. The funny "gotcha" one-liners seem to be the goal of conversations and even relationships.

And I think I know what could solve this problem—show respect.

Show respect to everyone you meet starting with your family members. Show respect to the neighbors, the postman, the store clerks, the grocery boy who helps carry out your groceries. And do it consciously, on purpose. Make it a habit.

I find if you behave civilly to those you meet, they treat you civilly also.

And I like that.

There's a lot that is wrong in this world, and some of it will never change. But we can change our little corner of it by showing respect and appreciation for those around us.

I'm Walter Furley, and that's how I see it.

Shaving

18 February 2009

I'm Walter Furley, and this is how I see it.

I hate to shave. It is such a tedious exercise, and after I'm done and dressed, I often find a spot I missed on the chin or the jaw. And every now and then, there is a nick that will start bleeding after you put on a white shirt.

I also hate to buy new razor blades. I bought one with a small supply of blades, but when I went to the store for replacements, I couldn't remember the name of the razor in my medicine cabinet. And actually bought the wrong blades, then had to go back to buy the right razor later, all of which was infuriating.

Then, the razor companies began making multi-blade razors. If one blade can give you a shave, what must two blades in the same razor do? An intriguing question. The answer is, it does the same as one blade but more expensively.

You'd think that answer would be the end of it, but no! Out comes a new razor with three blades. I had to try it—same result. Then four blades and yesterday I saw a new razor with *five* blades. I can just see the manufactures at a sales meeting,"Hey, they bought the two blade thing, now try three. They bought it! Well, try four. Bingo! Now let's go for five!" And of course the cost per blade goes up accordingly if not geometrically.

I've considered giving up shaving and growing a beard, but those early stages of growth are very uncomfortable and leave you looking like something from a play by Beckett. I can't stand myself looking like that. My beard should make me look like a man in a Titian painting, or perhaps a European king. But I digress.

Razors are just a necessary evil. I should be grateful I don't have to use the one my father did, a straight edge which was sharpened on a leather strap, and the shaving soap was mixed in a heavy mug with his initials on it. The few times I've gone to the barber for a shave and sat tensely while he moved that enormous blade over my cheeks were not pleasant times, though the shave was nice, and the talcum powder gave a pleasant feel.

I'm going to use only the disposable single razors from now on. Let them come out with a six blade razor. They can keep it.

However, it might be worth trying, just once, maybe.

I'm Walter Furley, and that is how I see it.

Concert

23 February 2009

I'm Walter Furley, and this is how I see it.

Saturday night's concert by the Corpus Christi Symphony was one of the best of the season. It featured the winners of last year's International Contest held by the Corpus Christi Music Teachers Association—two teenagers from Russia, pianist Behzod Abduraimov and cellist Fedor Amosov, both nineteen years old.

Behzod looked all of fifteen as he shyly entered to play the Tchaikovsky first piano concerto, and some nearby audience members murmured, "Not the Tchaikovsky again." But from those first opening chords, the teenaged Russian had a grip on his audience and the piano and the Tchaikovsky that he would not let go. In fact after the first movement, the audience jumped to its feet and roared its approval and admiration. This when tradition calls for no applause until the end of the third movement. Young Behzod looked surprised and a little bewildered, and looked to the conductor as to what to do, and the conductor signaled him to rise and bow, which he had to do three times before the audience would let him continue. He was brought back three times for a curtain call.

Then the young cellist Fedor, who is six-feet four with brown curly hair and an angelic baby face, strode on stage, settled in, and began one of the most difficult of works, the Shostakovich "Cello Concerto No. 1." It mercilessly depicts the horrors of life under Stalin, with a second movement devoted to a virtual solo by the cellist, so soft and elegiac that we could almost hear sobs and weeping in his performance. Fedor played with all the passion and expertise of a Yo-Yo Ma.

Two young musicians who floored their audience and deserve world recognition. Yet, I spoke with one of the judges for this year's concert who commented that it doesn't matter how good or great a performer is, he will never make it professionally without marketing. In other words, someone must tell the world how good these young people are before the world will come to hear them.

And that is where the Corpus Christi Music Teachers Association comes in. This contest with top prizes of $5,000 and more has the attention of the whole music world. Contestants enter from China, Korea, Europe, and yes, Russia. A winner of this competition has a good chance of winning others, such as the

Van Cliburn Competition in Ft. Worth, or the Tchaikovsky competition in Moscow, and with such acclaim can earn a prestigious performance tour or a recording contract. This year's contest just ended with two more such winners, which we hope to hear with the Symphony next year. It's great step above "American Idol," and the Corpus Christi Music Teachers can be proud of their very hard work in the contest.

I'm Walter Furley, and that's how I see it.

Dandelions

27 March 2009

I'm Walter Furley, and this is how I see it.

You know, dandelions are really pretty when you stop and look at the little blossoms. One sprang up near my outside faucet this week, a lovely circle of brilliant yellow with hundreds of pure white petals surrounding it like white fur around a yellow disc. It just appeared there, furtively, in the moist earth beside the house in a place were hardly anyone would ever see it, except when we would turn on the faucet to water the garden. It seems an unusual dandelion, for most are all yellow and grow on large ungainly stalks with prickly leaves. These are the ones I avidly pull up, dig up, or chop up.

And I must admit dandelions look lovely when they go to seed with that bubble of feathery seeds hovering on the stalk waiting for a slight wind to scatter them all over my yard and my neighbors' yards to grow and choke out grass and other flowers. The seeds look almost fairy-like as they sail through the air oblivious to any gravity and seem to joyously, or mischievously, cover the earth with the plant's progeny.

There must be some good in dandelions. I hear some gourmet diners pick the leaves of the young plants and eat them in salads. I've never done that, to my knowledge. (Have you ever wondered what is in those packages of "field greens" we buy at the grocery store?)

My grandmother told of how in northern Louisiana, she would go into the woods and look for a plant called "poke," which she said was similar to dandelions. And her family loved to eat "poke" salad.

But she never picked dandelions for some reason.

If one doesn't watch them, dandelions can clump up and virtually destroy a nice lawn or flower bed. After I have tried to pull up all I find on my property, I see other lawns in the neighborhood with flourishing dandelions and wonder if I would be breaking trespass laws by walking over and pulling up the spiky green stalks.

Even so, I admit the yellow dandelion flowers are very pretty, and might even look good in an arrangement, though I doubt I'd ever buy one. Dandelions have their place in the scheme of things, I suppose. I just wish they weren't so very prolific.

I'm Walter Furley, and that is how I see it.

English
23 April 2009

I'm Walter Furley, and this is how I see it.

A friend sent me an E-mail this week I feel compelled to share with you. It reveals some elemental truths about our language.

Let's face it. English is a crazy language There is no egg in eggplant, nor ham in hamburger; neither apple nor pine in pineapple.

English muffins weren't invented in England or French fries in France.

Sweetmeats are candies, while sweetbreads, which aren't sweet, are meat. We take English for granted, but if we explore its paradoxes, we find that quicksand can work slowly, boxing rings are square, and a guinea pig is neither from Guinea nor is it a pig.

And why is it that writers write, but fingers don't fing, grocers don't groce, and hammers don't ham?

If the plural of tooth is teeth, why isn't the plural of booth, beeth?

One goose, two geese. So...one moose, two meese? One index, two indices? Doesn't it seem crazy that you can make amends, but not one amend? If you have a bunch of odds and ends and get rid of all but one of them, what do you call it?

If teachers taught, why didn't preachers praught?

If a vegetarian eats vegetables, what does a humanitarian eat?

Sometimes I think all the English speakers should be committed to an asylum for the verbally insane. In what language to people *recite* at a play, and *play* at a recital? Ship by truck and send cargo by ship? Have noses that run and feet that smell?

How can a slim chance and a fat chance be the same, while a wise man and a wise guy are opposites? You have to marvel at the unique lunacy of a language in which your house can burn up as it burns down, in which you fill in a form by filling it out, and in which an alarm goes off by going on.

English was invented by people, not computers, and it reflects the creativity of the human race, which of course, is not a race at all. That is why when the stars are out, they are visible, but when the lights are out, they are invisible.

Oh, and just out of curiosity—why doesn't *Buick* rhyme with *quick*?

I'm Walter Furley, and that is how I see it.

Omphaloskepsis

17 May 2009

I'm Walter Furley, and this is how I see it.

One of my recent rantings was on big words, one of which was omphaloskepsis, a big word meaning self-absorption or contemplation of one's navel. One listener knew the word and used it quite casually in a group conversation strictly for my benefit, and a doctor asked for a definition. When told, he said, "Of course. The *omphalos* is the Greek word for navel. In fact there is a mountain in Greece named Mt. Omphalos, and it is called the 'navel of the world.'"

Stunning information, you must admit, though it is apparently useless in normal life. Still, I was impressed, not only by the fact that I had used the word on the air, but that someone had heard it and remembered it, and that a practicing physician enlarged upon it.

Since then I have been intrigued by the idea. How does one contemplate one's navel. Lying down, of course, it would be impossible, unless you used a mirror. Sitting up, one would have to lean forward uncomfortably and then get only a partial view. But why on earth would one do that? I remember in junior high gym class, we were quite conscious of our navels—some poked out, some sank in, so we called them "innies" and "outies," and had some strong opinions as to which were preferable, as though we had a choice.

The navel is the last connection with our mothers at birth, of course, and her navel was her connection with her mother, on and on back generations to the beginning of time. So it gives one a moment to think of being a continuum of life itself right there in the belly button. I've seen some people who have such a regard for it, they have it pierced and insert some rings or jewelry, which seems ostentatious if not unhealthy, jeweled *omphalos*.

The whole idea has made me nervous and wary. I must be very careful what words I use in these broadcasts. Someone listening may get inspired or stimulated to resort to omphaloskepsis.

I'm Walter Furley, and that's how I see it.

Accents

20 May 2009

I'm Walter Furley, and this is how I see it.

One of my favorite TV channels is the Texas Cable News, where news from the major cities in Texas is re-broadcast. When reporters go out into the field and interview people who live there, you notice a strong difference in accents, even here in Texas. Folk who live in rural areas near Dallas and the Panhandle have a definite Texas accent, the kind you hear satirized in cartoons and movies. You hear long drawn out diphthongs and a certain nasal quality, all of which is charming in its own way but very distinctive. Southern accents like those in Georgia and the Gulf Coast states take some acute attention when words like "oil" is pronounced "all" as in "olive all" or "do you wantcher all checked."

Comedians like Rich Little can pick up on vocal habits like these and perform them perfectly. His ear is unerring in his imitations of President Nixon or Reagan, and many others. He is so good it, one wonders what his real voice sounds like.

I believe we all are like Rich Little. From our birth we listen to those around speak and end up imitating them. Our parents, our siblings, our school mates all are models of our speech, and we pick up the sounds we hear from childhood on until our tongues, our throats, our minds are molded, imprinted with those sounds, so that when we speak, we are imitating all the speech we have heard all our lives.

We are a living example of our family, our community, our part of the country with every word we utter.

I was made painfully aware of this when I went to the University of Texas speech classes. My first class was a recording of myself reading an exercise that included all the possible speech errors the human voice could commit. That was in 1948, the first year the school had tape recorders for speech lab work.

I was utterly chagrined to think I sounded like that and was told that if I didn't lose that Texas accent, I would flunk the course. So, each class was spent on eliminating all those drawls, diphthongs, and dropped consonants. We were aiming for the NBC Midwestern accent, which NBC thought was the accent that offended the least people. Brooklyn accents, southern accents, western accents all were ridiculed by somebody somewhere. Well, I passed the course, even made an A, but in so doing, lost any real identity with my home state. I had to deny the accent my parents gave me, the one I shared with school mates and all those in my community, just so I could qualify to be a radio and TV announcer. If I sound as if I regret it, I don't. In fact, I just wish everybody would take the same course and try to speak more distinctly. I know I could understand them better.

I'm Walter Furley, and that's how I see it.

D-Day

6 June 2009

I was very moved by the observances of D-Day this year. The President and some European leaders gathered at Normandy to note the thousands of Allied troops who stormed ashore to begin the deadly campaign to drive the Nazis from France. Many of those present were white-haired and elderly, and they needed no occasion to remember the terrible time. The young people there were visiting the graves of their fathers or grandfathers or other relatives, young people whose only view of the event was the thousands of white crosses at St. Cloud and the grainy newsreel shots of the landing. They couldn't experience the horrendous roar of battle, the murderous machine gun fire raining down on the beaches where the brave troops were trying to run ashore. So their view of the war is as a spectator at an exciting event.

World War I was supposed to have been the war to end all wars.

But only those who fought in it and survived its horror really believed that. Enough people in the next generation thought war was the answer to everything and World War II burst forth to repeat the same horrors and devastation and millions of deaths.

So now it's been another generation since D-Day, and the world is facing another war. It's being fought far away now, but everyday it seems to be coming closer. So this generation is facing its own war, oblivious to all the wars before that were supposed to teach is all such grave lessons.

It's as though we refuse to learn just what war really is.

Shakespeare said, "He jests at scars that never felt a wound."

And a wonderful Pete Seeger song says "Where have all the soldiers gone? Gone to graveyards every one. When will they ever learn? When will they ever learn?"

Those who have learned are gone to graveyards every one. And the few who remember it all to well are decreasing in number every day. Those who never felt a scar seem to be saying, "Let's have a war." Peace seems to bore them.

Wars are usually fought because someone wants what another has and tries to take it by force. It may be land or territory, riches in the land, or just control of a land or people and quite often all of the above. It was true of the Greeks, the Romans, the Normans, the Mongolian hordes, the European empires, on and on. But please! We don't need another war. Listen to those who have lived through one, and think of those who died.

I know that's a pessimistic view, but when will we ever learn?
I'm Walter Furley, and that's how I see it.

Digital Changeover

19 June 2009

I'm Walter Furley, and this is how I see it.

Well, television has now changed over from analog to digital, and while the pictures do seem clearer, I'm not sure the content has changed at all. At least not for the better. Comedy shows still rely on comedy sex, as though sex were another form of entertainment rather than a form of real human relationships. News programs seem to have little censorship, showing criminals making obscene gestures at the camera, lots of blood and gore and violence, sometimes preceded by a gratuitous warning that the video will be "graphic," which instead of warning us to look away, makes us watch all the more intently.

I began my career in television right when television itself was beginning. All video was black and white, and most of it was live meaning what you saw was happening right then. News shows were live with some film and slide illustrations. Studio shows like "Ed Sullivan" and "Milton Berle" were live. Soap operas were live. Commercials, especially local commercials, were live. If you saw someone talking about a sale at Woolco, someone was live in the studio performing the spot live.

Some of the comedy shows were filmed, many before a live audience, but more often with a recorded laugh track that left you wondering what in the world the audience was laughing at.

The video was all black and white and seemed to be a real miracle in itself until color TV came along. The real miracle for us in the industry was the invention of video tape. We could record at our convenience and telecast it on any schedule.

I think program content was much better then. Shows like "Mayberry RFD," "Father Knows Best," "The Danny Thomas Show," even "I Love Lucy" all maintained family values and decency and were genuinely funny. Newscasts showed respect for our president, even when the commentators disagreed with them. There was a dignity about everything on TV that is in short supply today.

Also there is a loss of great cultural programs, "Leonard Bernstein and the New York Philharmonic" on Sunday afternoons, "Playhouse 90," "Dave Garroway," and "Omnibus," which was the first to use live feeds from various parts of the country. Today, I can only give thanks for KEDT and PBS for continuing that quality of television.

So television is actually repeating itself. When it was invented, it was the greatest communication tool we've ever known. But we weren't sure what to communicate. Today, we have a picture quality far better than ever, but still, we are looking for something worthwhile to say and show. Meanwhile, it's something to entertain until something new, if not better, comes along.

I'm Walter Furley, and that's how I see it.

Rat

15 July 2009

I'm Walter Furley, and this is how I see it.

My wife and I may be breaking a law. She is now feeding four stray cats that showed up begging in our yard, plus two neighbor cats who like the food. Two of them came as mother cats. After the kittens were given away to friends, the mothers were taken to the veterinarian for fixing. With that problem solved, we were faced with two more cats, but they turned out to be males and are very territorial and seem to be keeping other cats away. So at the moment the population count is constant.

I'm not sure about the legal limit for cats. Even so, I find the cats annoying. The trip to the grocery store always includes a generous collection from the pet food aisle, both dry cat food and canned cat food. And the accumulation of empty cans is astounding and must surely cause wonder among the recycling crew. The irony is both I and my wife are allergic to cats. Two will sneak into the house when we are not looking and hide. We are not aware until we begin sneezing and rubbing our eyes, and then have to begin a search under beds and in closets to find them and put them out. Every day I say, "We have to get rid of those cats."

But yesterday, I opened the back door to find a large rat, dead and lying neatly on the doormat. It was as big as a kitten and had fresh puncture wounds around its neck, obviously executed by one of our cats. I looked at them, and they lay languorously on the patio floor looking up at me with what could have been a look of pride. Now up until a few years ago, we were bothered by rats and mice in the garage, and we suspect in the attic. But we called an exterminator and thought *we* solved the problem. We've not seen a rat in years, until yesterday.

So I have tempered my annoyance with the cats. I no longer see them as ne'er-do-wells sleeping all day except for meal times. I see them as guardians of the domicile. They stalk the entire yard, climb trees to the roofs of the house and garage, and generally keep the entire area in their control.

So hooray for cats! Now if only they could keep away the awful grackles that swoop down to get the extra cat food. The cats just lie there and look at those ugly black birds, as though they weren't worth the trouble of chasing. But we all have flaws, don't we?

I'm Walter Furley, and that is how I see it.

Cronkite

20 July 2009

I'm Walter Furley, and this is how I see it.

The passing of newsman Walter Cronkite has stirred the memories of all America. He is especially remembered by many of us here in Corpus Christi. Cronkite credited the owner of KZTV, Channel 10, Vann M. Kennedy with giving him his first job. Mr. Kennedy headed the Austin branch of the International News Service, and Cronkite was a student at The University when Kennedy hired him as a student reporter. In his biography, Cronkite devotes several pages to the things he learned from him about practicing journalism. It was an association that lasted the rest of Cronkite's life. After his graduation, he credits Kennedy with getting him a job on the *Houston Chronicle*. He moved on to other papers, ending up in Washington as a cub reporter for United Press.

When the Texas Association of Broadcasters honored Mr. Kennedy as a broadcast pioneer, Cronkite came to Corpus Christi to deliver the keynote speech. In it he said when he first went to Washington, he kept running up against closed doors, unable to gain an interview from anyone. He called Mr. Kennedy for advice. Now Mr. Kennedy had been head of the Texas State Democratic party in the 30s, a time when Texas had several prominent men in national government. Cronkite says Mr. Kennedy told him to go see Sam Rayburn, Lyndon Johnson, Vice President John Nance Garner, and others and tell them he brings greetings from Vann Kennedy in Texas. Cronkite said it worked. He so impressed United Press with his Washington connections, he was made their first reporter to cover World War II in Europe, and as they say, the rest is history.

Cronkite also returned to Corpus Christi to speak at a fund raiser for Spohn Hospital. The hospital knew of the Kennedy-Cronkite connection and asked Kennedy to inquire about inviting the newsman to speak. Cronkite accepted, but said his manager required a $50,000 fee. The hospitals gained over $200,000 for the event, and after the speech, a hospital officer announced that Walter Cronkite had donated his $50,000 fee to the hospital. True to his nature, Walter Cronkite showed class—real class.

During his trips to Corpus Christi, Cronkite would visit Mr. Kennedy at KZTV, and Cronkite insisted on seeing the newsroom where I was the editor. He was quite affable with all us reporters, treated us as equals, and even graciously posed for a picture with us. As I said, what ever he did, Walter Cronkite showed class—real class.

I'm Walter Furley, and that is how I see it.

Grackles

3 August 2009

I'm Walter Furley, and this is how I see it.

Can anyone say anything good about grackles?

They look dirty, they sound awful, and they leave a mess wherever they perch or roost. The ones in my neighborhood must have a serious gastrointestinal condition. My newly washed car has white splashes all over it.

What do the darn things eat? I've never seen them chase mosquitoes or looking for worms and grubs. So far, I've seen them eat only cat food. I somehow thought cats would frighten them away, but our cats do not seem to mind sharing one bit. What's worse, the grackles will pick up the hard dry cat food, go dunk it in the cat's watering dish, then eat the water-softened pellets. Actually their ingenuity is impressive, except they end up leaving my patio with huge white spots. My patio chairs are unusable after a grackle's visit.

I spent a whole afternoon and a whole bottle of Clorox to clean the chairs last weekend, and now....

Grackles look so ungainly, their long legs stomping as they walk, their long necks craning about keeping an eye on you and the cats and most of all, the cat food.

And I thought birds were supposed to sing! Grackles cackle or maybe they are saying their name. At any rate they make a grating noise that is at best irritating, at worst offensive. At times hundreds of them gather in the neighbors trees and keep up their cacophony for hours. No wonder some people have used shotguns on them.

As ugly as they look stalking about the patio for food, they do look beautiful when they fly. Their sharp beaks raised high, their tail feathers fanned out, and their long wings held like a ballet dancer's arms all make a beautiful image. They look like those artificial birds women used to wear on their hats. If only grackles would just keep on flying until they are gone, they might be tolerable.

But until then, don't they have any natural predators? I occasionally see dove feathers in my yard where one of the cats has feasted but never any grackle feathers. That's probably because they are not tasty even to cats. Nature likely created grackles for a purpose, but so far I've not been made aware of it.

I'm Walter Furley, and that's how I see it.

Haircut

19 August 2009

I'm Walter Furley, and this is how I see it.

It's time for me to get a new haircut. I can't remember when I had my last one, but when the hair falls below my ears, I know it is time.

When I was a news anchor, a haircut every week was required to maintain the news anchor image. Now that I'm retired, I no longer feel that pressure. But still, I do not enjoy haircuts.

When I was a boy, my father would take me to the barber shop periodically when he was getting his own hair cut. The barber would set me on a board which lay across the arms of the barber chair, throw a much used cloth about me, and attack me with clippers. They weren't even electric clippers, but hand squeezed clippers that often nicked the scalp and rarely left an even cut so that the bangs that hung on my forehead tickled irritatingly. My mother would have to repair the damage when we went home, but neither she nor I were ever happy with my haircuts. The barber would then put a splash of something on my head from a bottle marked "Jeris," leaving a very fragrant smell that lasted the rest of the day, and sort of sweet, spicy smell. But I liked it and endured the haircut just to be sure I received a splash of it. There was always a big brush that dusted powder on my face and neck, but it never removed all the bits of hair that clung to my skin, creating an itch that stayed until I could wash everything away.

Back in the thirties that haircut cost 25 cents. Times have changed today. And in the sixties, when it became fashionable for a man to have his hair "styled," I succumbed to hair spray. This seemed very practical with the hair staying in place all day with no problem re-combing it every time the wind blew. I was all ready for the next newscast.

But in retirement, especially in yard work, the hair goes its own way, always to the detriment of my image. I end up looking like an old man who doesn't take care of himself. So it's a quick trip to the barber, who can magically restore that silhouette of a well-groomed gentleman. It takes a great deal of imagination on my part to ignore the wrinkles and spots on my face, but with squinting eyes I am back to being much younger, the friendly news anchor I've always wanted to be thanks to my barber.

I'm Walter Furley, and that is how I see it.

Cat and Sandal

7 September 2009

I'm Walter Furley, and this is how I see it.

I have a cat that loves to rub its cheeks in my sandals. They lie there empty on the patio, and the little cat goes up and lovingly rubs its cheeks on them. It's kind of endearing, as though the little thing adores the sandals I walk on. But I remember when I had a dog and walked him every morning and evening. I had to watch him carefully, because he would find something odious in the grass and vigorously rub his cheeks in it. One winter night this happened, and I had to pick him up, hold him at arms length, and get him into the house and a bathtub for a thorough bathing and drying with a hair dryer. At the time I should have been relaxing in my bed trying to go to sleep, I was playing dog groomer with a very angry attitude. So why did the dog rub his cheeks in the filth?

Why did my cat rub its cheeks on my sandals? Did my sandals smell to the cat the way the filth did to the dog? Does that mean I have smelly feet? This is very unnerving. If I go out in public wearing my sandals, are other people aware of whatever it was the cat liked?

There is a store in our neighborhood which I visit occasionally, and the owner keeps two cats there. They bask in the store windows and lie regally about the displays and frequently accept a pat on the head or a rub on the back. But when I visit, they follow me about sniffing my sandals and even the path where I walk. I and the store owner think it amusing. But, now—what is going on?

Do I quit wearing sandals or get rid of the cats?

I've heard of something you put in your shoes called "odor eaters." I wonder if I need some for sandals.

This is really a consternation.

I'm Walter Furley, and this is how I see it.

Computer Time

7 September 2009

I'm Walter Furley.

I'm always surprised and exasperated at how much time I spend at the computer. What begins as just a check of the E-mail ends up with over an hour just browsing.

E-mail alone can waste an hour. There is the junk mail, which for some reason, includes a number of sales pitches for Viagra. Even though I mark them for the junk file, new ones always arrive. What makes someone out there think I need Viagra? And even more insulting, many of the offers at addressed to my wife! Anyway, I've learned to recognize them by the E-mail titles and junk them quickly. Then there are the E-mails from friends who have found something on the Internet they want to share, often virulently political, but sometimes some very beautiful pictures and sometimes some very funny jokes.

But before you know it, you've spent far too much time at the computer while work you had planned for the day is delayed sometimes to the point of not getting done at all.

A former colleague persuaded me to sign up for Facebook because it would keep me in touch with our fellow workers. However he apparently connected me with the 300 or so people I have in my E-mail roster, and I am connected with far more people than I can handle. There must be a way to eliminate some of them, but I haven't learned it yet, so I am treated daily to what children are doing, what is for supper, weird contests that I refuse to participate in, and personal information about people I don't remember ever meeting.

However, some of them put in an album of their vacation pictures and that's often very interesting.

So, it's really too hot for yard work, and if you have to help with dusting, it's just a never-ending chore, and if you stay at the computer long enough, it's nap time. Meantime, life is just passing on by, and I am losing control of time.

Still I'm not turning off my computer.

I'm Walter Furley, and that is how I see it.

Rainbow

29 September 2009

I"m Walter Furley, and this is how I see it.

During a recent rain spell, I was driving down Ocean Drive, when the sun suddenly came out, and there was a moment of both sunshine and rain. Ahead of me a car was spinning up a heavy mist from the wet highway, and I was startled to see a rainbow on it. The rainbow followed the car for several moments until we came to a curve, and it was no longer in the proper angle for the reflection.

The rainbow was quite vivid and seemed to follow the car playfully giving the car a magical quality itself. The car was actually an old clunker, rusty, dented, and badly needing a new paint job. Well the analogies are obvious—beauty in strange places. But I was struck by the fact that I was probably the only one in the whole world who saw it. And I wouldn't have seen it had I not been looking at just that angle between the mist and the sun and at just that moment as the car sped on ahead of me.

The world is full of such moments, isn't it? Moments that we fail to see and fail to look for. How many sunrises and sunsets do we miss by sleeping late or fixing supper? How many friendly faces and greetings do we fail to see or acknowledge by being self-absorbed?

We all claim to be free, but actually we incarcerate ourselves in such narrow bits of life. We drive to work and get lost in our worries and fantasies and fail to see the trees that have turned greener, the new flowers that have blossomed, the wonderful color of the water in the bay. We may have left home without seeing some act of love from a wife or child.

There is a line in the play *Auntie Mame* in which she says, "Life is a banquet." And most of us just stand around looking at life and not enjoying it.

We miss a lot in our lives by not being aware, by not looking around us, by not seeing a rainbow in a surprising place.

I'm Walter Furley, and that is how I see it.

Vincent Sanders

29 September 2009

I'm Walter Furley, and this is how I see it.

I lost a friend a few weeks ago, a fellow choir member and singer.

Vincent Sanders was an unlikely man to be a singer. He was a large man, over six feet tall, perhaps a little ungainly, with a strong tendency to stutter when he spoke, though it never affected his singing. He sat beside me in the bass section of the church choir and proved to have a very good ear for the bass part of the choruses. But Vincent was not content to sing in just the chorus. He wanted to sing solos. Not surprisingly, he was very good at singing his Negro spirituals, and he sang them often in the First United Methodist Church to the great pleasure of the congregation.

I learned something from Vincent, I'm sure he never knew he taught me. I have always had a certain amount of stage fright in performing—singing, acting, speaking, even on a television news set. I've tried to analyze it: Am I afraid people won't like me? Will I forget my lines? Do I look all right?

Vincent never seemed to think of all that. Vincent loved to sing, and he loved his audience, and when he made his entrance with a big smile and sang, that audience loved him back. He wasn't begging for approval. He was showing how he loved being on that stage.

And that was the key. Don't fear your audience. Love your audience. Because the audience will give back what you give it.

Vincent did not look like the famous stage heroes, but when he sang "Old Man River," or "The Impossible Dream" he won us all over with a star performance. He sang in several other choirs in the city, appeared in musicals at Harbor Playhouse and other drama groups.

He even read stories to the children at Driscoll Children's Hospital.

So it was no surprise to see several hundred people attend his funeral, black, white, Hispanic, people from the whole spectrum of the community. I think they all had learned the Vincent lesson. Give love, show love in what you do, and you will have nothing to fear.

I'm Walter Furley, and that is how I see it.

Signatures

4 November 2009

I'm Walter Furley, and this is how I see it.

Writing one's signature has become a joke. As one whose education included penmanship classes, and poor handwriting on a theme would lower your grade, I wonder how many of the young people today made it through high school, much less college.

I've seen signatures that were nothing more than a squiggly line, no more legible than a chicken scratch.

I've always written my name proudly, trying to imitate the calligraphy on the Declaration of Independence, especially the John Hancock signature. I developed a special flourish for the letter "W," and the "F" in Furley is copied from the elegant trademark of the Fairmont Hotel. I think it would look at home among the signatures on the Declaration.

Not today's signatures. I've received correspondence from chief executives signed with an illegible scrawl. I wonder how a handwriting expert would interpret such writing. I've told my own son that if I had to testify in court about his signature, I could not do it. It looks nothing like his name.

It is alarming that penmanship is not taught in our schools today. Computers seem to take care of all forms of communication.

This is likely a relief to teachers who have to muddle through hundreds of theme papers each week. Bad handwriting could be a real chore to them.

In the Orient I understand each person carries with him a "chop" or a print block with the impression of his name. Inking and stamping it on a document is the same as signing a signature. This, in countries, where calligraphy is considered an art.

So what's the point. My carefully autographed checks whiz through a bank's computer no more appreciated than the poorly written ones. Every check is reduced to a computer read-out, so theoretically no signature is needed.

Handwritten letters are also rare today. I used to raise an eyebrow at typed personal letters, but at least the strike-overs and corrections showed the touch of a human hand. Letters written on a computer are always letter perfect, but if the sender's name is not printed on it somewhere, that streak of ink at the bottom would never reveal who wrote me the letter.

Bring back penmanship classes.

I'm Walter Furley, and that is how I see it.

Chrysanthemum

6 November 2009

I'm Walter Furley, and this is how I see it.

I've neglected my backyard garden and now the chrysanthemums have gone wild and run out of their bed and over the walkway, so that I can't get by without trampling them. The obvious answer is to take the clippers to them, but they are beginning to bloom. Thousands of little white mums bursting into blossom creating a whole bower of flowers languishing lazily on the walkway where they don't belong.

But they look so great and smell so good. They know they are going to stay there until the flowers are gone. Then a good haircut for those mums.

I'm sure you can tell by this that I am no gardener. I buy pretty plants at the nursery, stick them in the ground, and often watch them die. But sometimes they surprise me and actually grow. These mums were in the garden when we bought the house some thirty years ago, and they've never quit blooming, even when I cut them back severely.

So I admire their perseverance as well as their blossoms.

Another success is my row of amaryllis. A friend makes a point of giving us a bulb each Christmas. And after it blooms indoors, we set it out in the garden by the fence. We have over twenty now, and while you'd expect them to repeat the cycle and all bloom at Christmas time, they can bloom anytime from December to May, in spite of no attention from me. That's the way plants were meant to be—bloom on their own with none of my interference.

We have a single rosebush which we transplanted from another family home. It is doing very well. We read in the newspaper that putting used tea leaves around it will help fertilize it. So every morning after our tea, instead of putting it in the garbage, I put the tea leaves around the rose bush. Not so much result so far, but my wife has suggested perhaps I should take the tea out of the tea bags before throwing it under the rose bush. Oh oh. That's more work involved in gardening that I had anticipated. That's as bad as the overgrown chrysanthemums.

There's a reason why we shouldn't mess with Mother Nature.

I'm Walter Furley, and that's how I see it.

Bullying

9 November 2009

I'm Walter Furley, and this is how I see it.

I'm sure you still are as disturbed by the shootings at Ft. Hood as I am. But just as disturbing is the report that the shooter felt he was bullied by his fellow Army officers.

This man was an officer, trained in psychology, and whose work in the Army was to help military personnel who had psychological problems. That he couldn't counsel himself is beyond understanding.

But to learn that he had been taunted by others in the Army, even officers (and remember he was a Major himself), shows the extent of damage that can be done by bullying.

We remember what happened at Columbine High School when two students were taunted and ridiculed until they turned on the school with murderous gunfire.

It can even happen to a Major in the United States Army.

It shows that everyone—students, Major officers—everyone needs to be accepted by those with whom he works and lives.

To be rejected can result in hurts that can result in harm, in tragedy.

I wonder if those whom the shooters resented realized they were behaving like bullies, refusing to be friendly, or even speaking to them in a derogatory manner. Doing that takes some real effort. Being malicious takes premeditation.

On the other hand, a warm handshake or friendly greeting can come so easily and could be the very reassurance that would wipe away the brooding resentment that is obsessing people like the student attackers at Columbine or the enraged Army major.

So, for every brooding, resentful attacker there have to be those who failed to be friendly, failed to be aware of a person needing that support, even failed to give a smile of understanding.

Everyone needs approval. Everyone needs support. When approval and support are denied, the person is rejected, the person is insulted, and the person feels justified in striking out in revenge, maybe with a curse word, an obscene gesture, or a physical attack.

This sounds like what your mother tells you, but being nice to everyone is important. Who knows what good it can do. And who knows what evil can come if it is denied.

I'm Walter Furley, and that is how I see it.

Food Channel

17 November 2009

I'm Walter Furley, and this is how I see it.

I confess, I have become addicted to the Food Channel.

Actually, my wife became addicted first, and as is often the case in addictions, I began to share it.

We have different objectives, however. She is interested in the food and recipes and actually tries some out to various degrees of success.

But I have found the Food Channel to be a source of mindless relaxation. There is no mention of the wars, the voices are all light and friendly even happy at times, and the food always looks very enticing. When I focus my mind on these cooking shows, I experience a great feeling of comfort, relaxation, a real relief from any tension or worries I may have had. There's a new cook, or chef, every half hour so you don't get tired of any one of them, and you can sit there on a soft couch and let several half hours go by before you realize there are other things to do. And there is a great variety within the shows. None seem to be as sophisticated as Julia Child's, but all are so affable and friendly, you really think they are there just to talk to you. Performance wise, the Food Channel chefs have reached a new peak of audience communication. Some are from the south and say they specialize in good southern cooking, and they do it with a southern accent that is as thick as the butter and cream they use in their recipes. One specializes in Italian cooking, another in grilled food, another in quick meals, but all are so absolutely gleeful in cooking that they end up making you gleeful just watching them.

That's on the spectator aspect. It's appalling really that they pay no attention to healthy diets, but slather on pounds of butter, pour quarts of heavy cream, and insist on lots of fat in the meats they cook.

And some of the cooks show the results of their diets.

I am safe from all those recipes, however. First of all, those ingredients would break my budget to say nothing of my waistline. Second, the time and effort spent in preparing those dishes would require much more work than I would ever want to invest in a meal.

But just watching and listening can be a worthwhile endeavor.

Happy voices, speaking of happy things, with a display of beautiful things you would like to eat. It is much better for your mind and body than taking drugs. Just don't switch to the news channel too quickly. The shocking change may be too much.

I'm Walter Furley, and that is how I see it.

2010

New Car

14 January 2010

I'm Walter Furley, and this is how I see it.

I wonder if I'm the only one who is disappointed in the new car designs. They all seem to look alike, like a football with both ends cut off or like a fat bug racing down the highway.

I well remember my first car—a Ford Fairlane, four-door, blue on white, with wonderful lines on each side that looked like folded wings. Inside was a fine AM radio, and shiny vinyl seats. No air conditioner, probably because I couldn't afford it. Gasoline was 17 cents a gallon, so mileage was no problem. I proposed to my girlfriend in that car so remember it with great affection because she said "yes," partly I think because she liked that car, too. But it began having problems that were too costly to repair, so I sadly traded it in for something less loved. But it looked so great. And I thought I looked great in it. Not so today's cars. They seem to close in around you like a bubble, and the windows are tinted so no one can see you inside, and even the very expensive cars look like the economical ones from Korea.

However, inside is quite a different matter. Leather seats, a Geographic (sic) Positioning System, AM-FM radio, CD player, little screens that tell you the time, temperature, and what kind of mileage you're getting. And that's just the basic package. You can get all sorts of extras that seem to give you control of the universe as you drive.

But style is very lacking. I find no new car that looks as great as my first Fairlane. Style usually wins over substance. But why can't car designers give us both.

I'm Walter Furley, and that's how I see it.

Joolery
15 January 2010

I'm Walter Furley, and this is how I see it.

I thought I was losing my hearing when I first heard it, but after re-watching a particular TV commercial, I know I heard it right. There are people in this city who say: "JOO ler ee" for "JOOL ree."

They are talking about jewels, not jules, but they say "JOO ler ee."

I first heard this in New York City when I lived there for awhile. I dismissed it as a local aberration, like our "yawl" in the south. But here?

I have just about gotten used to so many people mispronouncing "nuclear" as "NEW-que-lər," assuming they had a handicap that could not be corrected.

But JOO ler ee?

I was watching a program on "Masterpiece Theatre," a story set in Victorian England, where everyone spoke properly, in well constructed sentences, using a vocabulary that is beyond any in our everyday conversations. I must say, I am glad we no longer speak that way, if ever people did.

But to mispronounce perfectly ordinary words means you have never learned how to say the words correctly. Have our teachers failed, or has television and radio corrupted us?

So what should we do? If we hear someone say JOO ler ee, should we respond with "do you mean jewelry?" and risk being labeled a pedantic, or a snooty person, and be avoided by those we are trying to help?

Well, I suspect we are all just about as smart as we want to be, and don't want anyone to change us.

So, JOO ler ee is just another thing we will have to endure. After all it is a free country.

I'm Walter Furley, and that is how I see it.

Wine

2 March 2010

I am Walter Furley, and this is how I see it.

I fear I have some kind of defect or aberration because I do not like wine. It seems we are supposed to be predisposed to like wine. Look at all the poems and literature praising it. It's even admired in the Bible. But all I have ever tasted tastes like fruit juice that went bad. Wine is simply not delicious.

Once I was served a glass of Mogen David wine. It was very sweet and I rather enjoyed it, but it could not compare to a glass of fresh squeezed orange juice or even grape juice. At parties when wine is served, I hesitate to refuse thinking I will be regarded as judgmental, so I nurse one goblet throughout the evening, thinking I am blending in with the party and contributing brilliant conversation and amusing anecdotes. But I could do that without the wine. There is just some sort of peer pressure to hold on to a very pretty wine glass as you share in the gathering.

I've read of people paying thousands of dollars for a bottle of wine, wine which is often many years old, some even a hundred years old. I've yet to hear of the bottle being opened, or if the 100-year-old wine tastes any better than last year's vintage from California.

And the price of wine is so varied. My grocery store features it from around five dollars a bottle to twenty and thirty dollars. I've even seen one with a price tag of $248. How on earth could a liter of any liquid be worth that? Water in the desert perhaps.

Now part of my resistance to liking wine may lie in my Texas Hill Country upbringing. In Sunday school, the evils of all drink were vividly emphasized. And the summer church revivals back in the thirties featured preachers who told horrific stories of the tragedy brought by alcohol. The result was that for years I found it difficult to believe that perfectly good people could drink beer and even wine. But putting that aside, I just do not find the taste of wine inviting. I do not think the less of you for enjoying it, but I frankly don't see why you do. A glass of Dr. Pepper would be just as enjoyable.

I am Walter Furley, and that is how I see it.

Telemarketers

5 March 2010

I'm Walter Furley, and this is how I see it.

I wonder how effective telemarketing really is. During the last election campaign, my telephone rang with messages from politicians, all pre-taped, all delivered with the urgent sales pitch used in television commercials. All annoying, and all were hung up on before the message ended.

My telephone is much like my front door. If you call me and come visit me, you are entering my space, using my time to impart information often to persuade me to participate in or support a cause in which I have limited interest. And I resent it. As a consequence, I make extensive use of Caller ID, and if the party is unknown or the number is out of my area, I just do not answer.

Likely I miss some calls I would like to answer, but so far I've not been aware of them. I've had my telephone number listed on the Do Not Call Registry, but somehow some calls come through anyway.

I think most people reject and resent such calls. The telephone is a personal service we have contracted for and are paying for and should not be at the disposal of those who want to make us targets, or even victims.

So why do telemarketers persist? Evidently someone answers them, even succumbs to their solicitations. So perhaps one success out of twenty-five failures is cost productive.

It's the same process with junk mail, except the people doing the mailing have to pay postage for the privilege of loading my mail box. And I confess some of such mail is interesting, and I even use some of the coupons, but most goes right into the wastebasket or the recycling bin.

Junk mail I can live with. But when you're on my telephone, you are getting very personal, and I don't let just anybody do that. Call me to wish me happy birthday or to tell me company is coming, but don't call to sell me something.

I'm Walter Furley, and that is how I see it.

Coliseum

26 March 2010

I'm Walter Furley, and this is how I see it.

The disposal of Corpus Christi Memorial Coliseum seems to be on the minds of everyone in town. Should we tear it down to make way for a revamping of Shoreline Boulevard, or should we maintain it as a memorial to those local citizens who died in World War II?

Memorials, no matter how fervently they were built, are an impermanent thing. The Civil War memorial on the Bluff at the end of Peoples Street stands ready to remember those who fought in that war, but how many go to visit to remember or even think of it as they drive by?

Bayview Cemetery beside IH-37 in Hillcrest was created to remember those who died in Zachary Taylor's army during its stay in the mid-1800s. It is rarely visited and often is overgrown with weeds and trash until some observant citizen organizes a cleanup.

The World War II memorial on the Bluff at Mesquite and Schatzel Streets was built to remind us of those who died in the War to End All Wars. The eternal flame installed there no longer burns, and most residents don't even know the small park exists.

The great, lavish memorials such as those in Washington, and at Arlington give us pause, but how often do we visit them. Just how remembered are all the dead who defended this nation with their lives?

We should not build memorials and then forget them. We should remember those who sacrificed, so that we might live by living the kind of life they died for, a life free of the hatred and the selfishness and the exploitation that started all the wars in the first place.

Those who died cared enough for us to assure us peace and safety. We who are living should care enough to work for the same.

So even though the Coliseum is a memorial, it means nothing if we continue to be in conflict with each other, to exploit each other, even to kill each other.

To really remember those heroes, we should have no crime in the city, no hunger, no homelessness. Those dead tried to leave us such a world, but do we remember? Do we need a statue or building to remind us? We need only one thing—a mirror so we can look into our own faces each day.

I'm Walter Furley, and that is how I see it.

Geranium

26 March 2010

I'm Walter Furley, and this is how I see it.

My geraniums are blooming! Not only are they blooming, but they are blooming spectacularly—multi-blossoms of the reddest red with leaves of the greenest green almost shout out loud about how great they look. Even the spicy smell of the geranium leaves are invigorating. Just a glance at the plant brings a look and a feeling of real pleasure.

Geraniums have played a large role in my growing up. As a child I remember Aunt Emma who seemed to be able to grow anything with easy success. She had hollyhocks along her fence, snap dragons and zinnias in front of them, and a border of little pink and white flowers mixed with blue bachelor buttons. And in the center of her yard was an apricot tree that bore fruit abundantly. But all this paled in comparison to the many pots of geraniums she set along the edge of her porch. Red, red, red with the big green leaves. Just the thought of them delights me as much as daffodils delighted Wordsworth.

I have tried growing geraniums previously.

Well I would buy geraniums at the nursery or even the grocery store, and wonder why they didn't look like those of Aunt Emma, or even survive the summer as hers did.

Geraniums like many things are fleeting and will not last forever no matter how much I water, fertilize, or cultivate. So when I do find a successful burst of red and green, I cherish it for the brief time it lasts. A pot full of geraniums can just make any day so much better.

I'm Walter Furley, and that's the way I see it.

Orion

26 April 2010

I'm Walter Furley, and this is how I see it.

My favorite constellation has set in the west and will not appear until midwinter next year. Orion is one of the easiest constellations to identify, after the Big Dipper, but is also the most beautiful.

In the center is a line of three smaller looking stars that are called "Orion's Belt" and stretching from them are two larger stars at each end. One of them has marvelous name, "Betelgeuse," which I love to say. Betelgeuse. It has a rather plain meaning, "hand of the giant." The other star is "Bellatrix," meaning "female warrior," which seems appropriate. Bellatrix.

At the other side of the belt are Rigel, which sounds like an English movie star, and Saiph, s-a-i-p-h, which sounds like nothing but means "sword." Rigel means foot.

The astronomy books say the three stars in the belt are all around a thousand light years away, which means the light we are seeing now was emitted at the time of the crusades, when the Mayan civilization was thriving in Mexico, and other ancient activities were forming our civilization.

In looking at Orion I am awed at what I cannot see with my naked eye, the Horse Nebula, a huge cloud of cosmic dust that forms the silhouette of a horses head, seen only with a giant observatory or the Hubble telescope.

And Orion takes up only a small portion of the sky. There is so much to see, it is beyond our comprehension. The stars were all named by Arab astronomers, who must have spent many dark nights in the cold desert, admiring the same stars I watch now. Scientist say our very bodies are composed of the very elements in the stars, the chemicals, the minerals, the gases scientists see up there.

That's an awesome thought. I am made up of the same thing as Orion. Even though it has set in the western sky, I know Orion is there and will come again to visit next year. Orion and I are friends, great friends.

I'm Walter Furley, and that is how I see it.

Pun

26 April 2010

I'm Walter Furley, and this is how I see it.

I've always loved puns, even bad puns, but a friend gave me a list of some great ones recently, and I can't resist sharing them with you, or maybe I can't resist saying them aloud.

Here's the first one, so listen carefully:

The famous Viking explorer, Lief Erikson, returned home from a voyage and found his name missing from the town register. His wife insisted on complaining to the local civic official who apologized profusely saying, "I must have taken Leif off my census."

Now try this one:

There were three Indian squaws. One slept on a deer skin, one slept on an elk skin, and the third slept on a hippopotamus skin. All three became pregnant. The first two each had a baby boy. The one who slept on the hippopotamus skin had twin boys. This just goes to prove that the squaw of the hippopotamus is equal to the sons of the squaws of the other two hides.

Just one more, so hold on.

A skeptical anthropologist was cataloging South American folk remedies with the assistance of a tribal *brujo* who indicated that the leaves or fronds of a particular fern were a sure cure for any case of constipation. When the anthropologist expressed his doubts, the *brujo* looked him in the eye and said, "Let me tell you, with fronds like these, you don't need enemas."

Okay, okay, they are terrible puns, but I think they're funny.

I'm Walter Furley, and that's the way I see it.

New Dog

24 May 2010

I'm Walter Furley, and this is how I see it.

We have new dog at our house.

We've had myriad dogs and cats for some 40 years, but when the last ones died at some 15 and 19 years of age, we decided we had served and survived our last pets.

Then a friend called. She had an extra pet that did not get along with her other pets, could we possibly take her. Of course, we said "No," but she asked us to at least look at the dog.

So we have a new dog in the family. She is small, about six pounds, very demonstrative in greeting you when you come home, bouncing and barking and wiggling. She very effectively makes us feel loved and wanted. She apparently can't stand being apart of us, sitting right next to us as we read or watch TV, often getting into our laps every time we sit down. And sleeping—she either thinks she is another person or we are also dogs because she insists on sharing the bed also, curling up right next to us, sometimes where the knee bends, or if we are our side, she sneaks right into the waistline and gets very, very warm. I've found it advisable not to sleep on my back, for she climbs up on my body to use it for a bed, and often creeps up on my chest to awaken me with a wet tongue in my face. Actually, that part of her company is rather pleasant and endearing.

But she demands a walk every morning and every evening and sometimes in between. Since retiring, I have enjoyed a new habit of sleeping until 8 a.m. or so. But she is bouncing on and off the bed at 6:30. Knowing the result if I delay too long, I manage to crawl out of bed, get dressed in something presentable, and take her walking.

No, she takes me walking, straining at a leash wanting to go much faster than I, stopping abruptly to investigate new smells and stopping so quickly I sometimes almost step on her, this when I am not yet awake. There are two things I must make sure she accomplishes on each walk, and usually she does them both. But the incessant sniffing and searching out of the perfect spot to leave a calling card is exasperating. She is in control. Dog trainers say we must assert ourselves to show we are the alpha dog, but when she is walking she knows she is. The two walks a day I hope are good for me, because I am finding a growing resentment of them. While they have taken me off my couch to see a new moon form and see the early dew grow in the grass and see how the neighbors keep their lawn so much better than mine, I would really prefer to stay on the couch and get the latest from CNN or watch "Masterpiece Theatre". If she just didn't need the walking, she would be a perfect dog.

I'm Walter Furley, and that is how I see it.

Tallow Trees

24 May 2010

I'm Walter Furley, and this is how I see it.

I remember back in the forties, many newcomers to Corpus Christi were bemoaning the lack of trees. These were Navy people from up north or construction people from everywhere, who claimed that back home they had many beautiful trees. But Corpus Christi had hardly any, unless you count palm trees, and the newcomers didn't see them as trees at all.

Well the Caller-Times listened to the complaints and arranged for various nurseries to supply the paper with hundreds of saplings, most of them Chinese tallow. We were told they grew quickly, offered a great deal of shade, and would really green up a neighborhood. So almost everybody in town went down the Caller-Times and accepted the gift of two or three young trees and brought them home to improve the landscape.

They were attractive trees, growing quickly, and did not require much water. But after they matured in two or three years, they presented their problems. It is this time of year when the tallow trees drop thousands of little curly things about three inches long, each with hundreds of little spikes that cover a sidewalk in one night. The spikes cling to your shoes, your clothes, and especially a dog's coat. Now, when the curly things first fall, they are soft and pliable. But leave them a day and they grow quite stiff and the spikes are quite hard and are uncomfortable to walk on in bare feet. But worse, later in the spring, the tree will shed it seeds which are in little pods as hard as steel with a strong point at each end. That can discourage bare feet quite quickly. And the seeds fall by the thousands. Sweep them up one morning, they refill the walk by night time.

Now I have had nursery people tell me tallow trees do not last more than twenty years. But these were planted in my yard when the house was built in the 60s, and each has trunks of immense girth and have reached a height of some fifty feet. To look at them, you'd call them really wonderful trees.

So as I sweep up the little curly things and the sharp-spiked seed pods twice daily, I must remember to thank the Caller-Times for giving us these free trees back in the 1940s. They have made Corpus Christi greener, if a little irritated each spring.

I'm Walter Furley, and that is how I see it.

Little Things
16 June 2010

I'm Walter Furley, and this is how I see it.

I have a found a great appreciation for little things that are new to me or at least never before known to me, that have become everyday necessities—little things, but really useful.

For instance: I want to thank the person who decided to round off the bottoms of canned goods, so they stack perfectly without falling over. The bottom part of the can is rounded out, so that it fits right into the top part with the conventional edge. So simple, yet so useful, especially when you are stacking cans of pet food in the pantry.

Then, there are the little fasteners now being sewn into men's trousers, a smooth little clip on the left side of the waistband and then a little bar on the right, so that they fit together so smoothly and no buttons to work with and no odd bulges in your waistline. I'm sure some great tailor devised that, but thank goodness all trouser makers have picked it up.

And I appreciate these bottles or drink containers shaped with one side indented so the bottle carries its own handle. Instead of trying to wrap your hand around a large, round bottle, there is a nice narrow space for your hand to grip and hold onto the container, easily held even if the bottle is large or covered with condensation in the refrigerator. So thoughtful of someone.

And I appreciate those metal clips you buy at office supply, metal springs opened with two wire prongs that hold things fast and firmly. And they are good for not only holding sheets of paper together, they will hold anything they'll fit on. During this last winter when we thought a freeze was due, they held cloth sheets together to make a tent to put over our prized plants in the garden. Nothing else would have worked as well.

And while I'm at it, I really appreciate answering machines. It's almost miraculous to come home and hear voices of people who have tried to reach you. And caller IDs alert you to telemarketers so you don't have to answer and hear their efforts to get your money.

It all makes you really appreciate technology.

I'm Walter Furley, and that is how I see it.

Moon and Venus

16 June 2010

I'm Walter Furley, and this is how I see it.

Did you see the new moon this month? It was so near to the planet Venus you almost thought they were going to collide. I was alerted to the event by "Star Date" here in KEDT and made a special effort to be outside right after dark, and there was the big show. The crescent moon is one of my favorite sights—that sliver of light that peeks around the right side of the moon and the ghostly look of the rest of the moon that is barely lit by earthshine. Remember the pictures of the Apollo crew on the moon looking back at Earth glowing like another moon?

And Venus seems to get brighter every night. When it sinks low toward the horizon, it is magnified by the atmosphere and looks like a large plane coming in for a landing. In years when Venus is closer, it is so large and so much brighter, some people have called the police reporting a UFO. One of the most beautiful arias in opera is in Wagner's "Tannhauser," written as a love song to Venus, the "Evening Star." It must be our most popular planet.

The following night, I went out to check on the moon and Venus, and they were much farther apart, of course. The crescent moon was a little larger and no longer the jewel-like curve when it was really a new moon.

As a boy growing up in the Hill Country, I remember my family being very aware of the new moon. Planting was governed by the moon phases. First quarter was good for some planting, half moon and third quarter for others. And apparently the system worked. We always had good crops of vegetables and fruit, except of course when the droughts came.

I don't remember much talk about Venus, however. Venus was the goddess of love, and her story didn't sit well in the Bible Belt.

But the moon will always be beautiful and always be there.

I'm Walter Furley, and that is how I see it.

Papaya

17 June 2010

I'm Walter Furley, and this is how I see it.

We lost our papaya tree this week. Papayas have thousands of seeds inside, so last year we and some friends decided to plant them. Many of the seeds sprouted, and two of them actually became fruit bearing trees. They grew quite tall, eleven to twelve feet, and produced dozens of papayas. Papayas left to ripen on the tree are sweeter than cantaloupes, but they do not last long. When they ripen, they should be eaten right away because they begin to deteriorate very quickly. So when we had over a dozen papayas ripening at once we became very generous with our produce. And we found that some people do not like papaya and after tasting them said thanks but no thanks.

Well, the trees were still healthy when last winter's freeze nipped us, and we thought they survived. But as the warmer days came on, we saw the tips of the leaves turning black, and the fruit falling to the ground. One of the trees was severely damaged by the frost and began to wilt, so we cut it down. But the other seemed sturdy enough until the windstorm in May. It was so sad to see the entire top if the tree crashed to the ground with its splendid display of graceful leaves and fruit the size of your fist ready to grow into delicious melons, all smashed to the ground. The remaining tree seems doomed, jutting in the air, naked and badly scarred.

We may try again. One papaya with its thousands of seeds could supply us with a forest, if we like. It takes a year for them to grow to fruit bearing size, but the taste of the fresh papaya is so great, it will be worth the effort. I've heard of people planting avocado seeds and harvesting a fine crop. Avocados taste best when ripened on the tree also, so that's a good incentive.

Farming must be a nerve-wracking occupation. Planting the seeds and watching things grow seems easy enough. Although with my experience with frost and drought and wind storms with only two trees, I'm not sure I could handle the strain managing a whole farm.

I'm Walter Furley, and that's how I see it.

Dove

18 June 2010

I'm Walter Furley, and this is how I see it.

The doves were cooing this morning, a whole choir of them all over the neighborhood singing the same song together. I wonder if they are singing to communicate with other doves or if they sing just for the joy of it.

A bird watcher told me once you could recognize the dove's song because it sounded as if it were saying, "Who cooks for you?"

When you listen closely, that phase fits the pattern of the dove's song. But there is a Mexican song, literally, that is called "Cu-cu Caroo" which fits it better and even sounds like the bird. "La Paloma" is a Mexican folk song that uses the rhythm of the dove's cry set to music.

We have several types of doves living in our neighborhood, the Mexican dove, the Mourning dove, and the Aztec dove. I am not sure which is doing all the singing my neighborhood, but they are most vocal in the morning and seem to keep it up all day until nightfall.

It's a soothing sound and makes you realize why the dove is regarded as the symbol for peace. And that's all over the world.

Even the Bible uses the dove as a symbol for God's voice in the story of the baptism of Jesus.

So it is very disturbing to find quite often dove feathers in my back yard,where a cat has feasted on a trusting, if unwary, dove. I never see sparrow feathers or grackle feathers, only dove feathers. And to further the tragedy, I hear doves mate for life, so the consumed dove has left a lonely companion to cry while a fat cat lies sunning itself on the grass.

I've been to weddings where white doves were released at the end of the ceremony, which I find incongruous. Weddings unite, not set free to go separate ways.

I was at a funeral once where the family told a story about a dove.

They were gathered preparing to enter the church for the funeral of their father when a white dove landed on the patio just outside the door. On impulse one member opened the door and approached the dove. It hopped on the boy's finger and he carried it inside for all to see. The dove looked about, seemed to look into the face of each one there, then calmly took flight out the door and away. The family stood there silently, feeling their father and just visited them for the last time.

Doves are very special birds. The cooing in the morning, no matter how loud, is always a comforting and welcome sound.

I'm Walter Furley, and that is how I see it.

Fighting Mockingbird

19 August 2010

I'm Walter Furley, and this is how I see it.

I was startled this morning to hear a strange bird call as I stepped out our front door. It sounded like a chirp, chirp, then almost a hiss or even a growl. It was repeated several times, and I felt it had a definite meaning. After locating the bird in the tree, I saw it was a mockingbird, a bird which makes melodious sounds over and over. Here it was making obviously angry, even aggressive sounds. Then I saw why.

Underneath the shrubs were two cats lying casually, looking bored, occasionally flipping their tails. The mockingbird took a sudden jump into the air and swooped down toward the cats, obviously targeting them. There were a few feathers nearby which I thought were dove feathers, gray with white borders, but then I realized mockingbirds are the same color. And I wondered if the cats had caught the mate of the vengeful bird in the tree. Or was there a nest somewhere nearby, and the bird was trying to scare off any potential predators?

The cats were wise enough to lie down under the protective shrubbery, and the bird was wise enough not to fly too close to make his protests. But there was a drama going on here the details of which were not obvious.

I identified with the mockingbird. I would protect my home and my family by keeping them away from danger. And I'm sure I would protest if someone endangered them.

And the cats? Well, I had petted them occasionally, but I find them less endearing now.

I hope the mockingbird can recover from whatever trouble he felt the cats caused him. Surely he will resume his concerts and sing as joyously every morning as he has in the past. If he can feel vengeful, perhaps he can also be forgiving. That's what we humans have to do. Maybe birds can learn from us. Or is it the other way around?

I'm Walter Furley, and that is how I see it.

Crackers

20 August 2010

I'm Walter Furley, and this is how I see it.

I know we shouldn't complain about little things, but little things can be just as frustrating as big things.

Take those little packages of crackers and wafers that come individually wrapped in cellophane. One should be able to simply tear off one end and take out the crackers and munch away, but no. Those ends may be just cellophane, but they resist any attempt to tear them, and after persistent tries, one ends up with a little bag of cracker crumbs.

I've even resorted to trying to tear them open with my teeth, which embarrasses my wife, and that doesn't always work. Neither does using a knife and fork. The package eventually yields up its contents, but only after great effort and frustration.

I think restaurants should provide little scissors along with the packages of crackers or helpfully cut them open when they are served. I know the ladies would appreciate it. And I even more, because the sight of a grown man struggling with little package of crackers is not an attractive one.

I have a similar problem with new CDs or DVDs. The cellophane wrapping on each is so tight and so thorough, I cannot find a spot that will let me break the seal. It takes a sharp kitchen knife to break into the package. So far I have not damaged any CDs or DVDs, but the possibility is always there.

Well, as I said, I shouldn't complain about little things, but it's the little things that spoil the bigger things, isn't it?

I'm Walter Furley, and that is how I see it.

Teachers

20 August 2010

I'm Walter Furley, and this is how I see it.

A conversation with a teacher recently left me troubled and alarmed.

We were talking about the TAKS and ACT Tests students must undergo every year. He said in his opinion, the test was not to determine what students learned but what the teachers taught.

If a teacher's students did poorly, the teacher was blamed and often had to forgo raises and promotions while the students were not held responsible at all. He said teachers were reduced to force-feeding students only the information required in the tests, rather than interesting them in broader aspects of a subject and inspiring the habit of learning itself.

He also pointed out that a teacher's control of a class was so limited that he had almost no authority. The most he could do was send a troubling student to the principals office. And the paperwork required each day and other procedures mandated by state law took not only most of the teacher's time but took away his enjoyment of his job. He was glad he had only one more year before he could retire with full benefits. What's more, he said if he had known what the teaching career would become, he would not have tried to become an educator. Worse, he would not advise any young people to go into the profession. This when more and more teachers are needed for more and more students.

He taught in a school in another city in a poor neighborhood, where parents were rarely involved in their child's education and staged ugly protests when their child got a low or failing grade.

The one saving grace he found in his work was the occasional very bright student who wanted to learn and gloried in getting all As. He said he had several like that, and he spent all his spare time helping them get scholarships, even to the point of taking a group of them on a tour of campuses in the northeastern states where most of them were accepted. But most of them could not afford the expense of living that far from home even with the scholarship. At the moment, he is trying to raise money to solve that problem, too. I think he is obviously a fine teacher, dedicated and caring, but discouraged by the education system.

I believe there are many teachers like him who want to be relieved of all the red tape and paperwork and left to teach and inspire students to learn.

It seems to me that schools are controlled too much by our legislators, who know little of education but a lot about making laws.

The answer should be: let the teachers teach, using their own teaching talent and expertise, and let the legislators provide the money to keep the schools open and educating.

I'm Walter Furley, and that is how I see it.

Mr License Plates

8 October 2010

I'm Walter Furley, and this is how I see it.

I find it amusing while in traffic to read the license plate of the car in front of me. Some of the most creative are the vanity license plates custom made for a price, expressing one's individuality like "Big Ma" or "PAID UP" or "TX BORN," or "TX A N M" and so forth.

But one that has intrigued me lately is the one beginning with the letters MR, Mister. And I begin thinking of the men I've know whom I called by their initials. MR A. would be Mr. Allen, who used to own a furniture store here, MR B. for Mr. Bails who managed a store where I worked as a teen, MR C. for Mr. Creighton who taught in my high school.

I am surprised there are so many license plates with the MR prefix, but each one can conjure up a name from my history or the name of someone I know now. People whom I likely would never have thought of or remembered had I not been playing the Mister game.

MR K. would be Mr. Kennedy, who owned the TV station where I worked, MR J. would be Mister Jacoby who manages KEDT. It's fun to fit names to the letters, and every name brings up a memory of that person and what they meant to you. You can almost relive your life, as the names come back to mind.

There is a surprising number of MR Fs, and I am surprised at how many MR Fs I have known. Mr. Fowler, a banker in Marble Falls where I grew up. He always had a pocket full of pecans, and he used a pocket knife to cut away the shells, and we children would stand around to see who would get the fresh nuts. Mr. Franklin, who owned a ranch near Llano, whose son was in college with me.

Mr. Frost, of the banking business, whom I met once in San Antonio.

But most of all. The MR F. reminds me of my dad, Mr. Furley, who is still remembered by many people here in town, strangers who often come up to me to tell me how they admired him. So of all the MR licenses, I always look for a MR F. It instantly makes me remember Dad, and I somehow think he is remembering me.

I'm Walter Furley, and that is how I see it.

House Numbers

8 October 2010

I'm Walter Furley, and this is how I see it.

House numbers in Corpus Christi are almost a lost attribute. Trying to drive down a street and simultaneously look for house numbers is not only inconvenient but dangerous. By all standards, the house number should be immediately obvious at a glance both day and night.

But no, some are hidden in dark corners of the entrance, some are arranged vertically on a post (often with one number missing), and some are in the same color of the house, so they do not stand out to us searching for them. I appreciate those homeowners who paint their house number on the curb, but I am frustrated when a car is parked over it.

Even worse are the business owners who display their name prominently with absolutely no street number. And if one is unfamiliar with the company and is searching for only a street number, good luck.

I had occasion to visit a business, unknown to me, and as I drove down the very busy street, slower than usual as I tried to find the number, I found myself testing other drivers' patience if not their road rage. There were not enough numbers to even tell which side of the street had even numbers or odd numbers. Luckily, the firm I sought had a prominent name sign, which I passed and had to double back to park there.

The inconsistency of numbering residences and business is a dangerous one.

Firemen looking for a house on fire might be able to spot it by flames, but a call to 911 would find police and ambulances driving back and forth searching for a number that can't be seen.

Surely we do not need an ordinance requiring house numbers to be displayed prominently. Wouldn't good sense dictate that? Though good sense has not prevailed in any number of problems we face today.

So I am left with the typical situation—seeing the problem, but not the solution. All I can do is make sure you can see my house number day or night.

If only everyone would do the same.

I'm Walter Furley, and this is how I see it.

Blind Pianist

10 October 2010

I'm Walter Furley and this is how I see it.

Saturday's Corpus Christi Symphony concert was an astounding event. The featured performer was a young man from Japan, called Nobu for short, who even though he was blind from birth, played the piano so well he won this year's Van Cliburn Competition.

His award winning performance had been seen on PBS this summer, and his performance for the Corpus Christi Symphony was one of the first since then. No surprise, the Performance Art Center at A&M Corpus Christi was almost sold out.

We all came expecting something wonderful, perhaps with a little skepticism, wondering if it really were all true.

It was true.

From the first crashing chords of the opening measures, Nobu proved he not only knew that concerto, he was its master. His hands flew over the key board playing running octaves from the bottom of the scale to the very top, all in perfect synchronization with the orchestra. Or perhaps Maestro John Giordano was in perfect sync with Nobu. The two made astounding music together.

Nobu had learned a vast repertoire of classical music, including many concertos, by listening to his teacher play them on the piano. The Tchaikovsky Number One is a very difficult concerto for anyone. It had to be a monumental task to learn it by ear, seeing no music score whatsoever. Most of us who try the piano have to look at the keyboard to see where to play. Nobu couldn't, of course, but it did not matter.

The evening was a real lesson in human achievement. Few of us face obstacles such as the blind Nobu, but we often fail to realize our potential, saying "it"s too much work," or make other excuses. But Nobu refuses to acknowledge an obstacle, and plays the world's most difficult piano works with apparent ease, though I know the thousands of hours he put in to learn the work.

I thought of something else Saturday night as I saw this Japanese young man playing a world class concert. This event could not have happened sixty-five or so years ago. Then we were fighting and killing Japanese, and the Japanese were fighting and killing us.

What a contrast from that bloody time of history to the beautiful evening before us the concert hall. Wars may destroy and kill, but look and listen to what peace has created. Nobu is the perfect example of how to make peace, not war.

In all the places in the world where war is being waged today, there are many other Nobus waiting and hoping to show the world what peace can bring.

I'm Walter Furley, and that is how I see it.

Guam

7 November 2010

I'm Walter Furley, and this is how I see it.

I had a friend tell me the most amazing thing recently.

There is a United States congressman who is concerned that the island of Guam may tip over and capsize if any more people are put on it.

Now think about that.

The Pentagon is considering moving 8,000 servicemen from Japan to Guam as part of the peace treaty made in 1945.

There is a military base on Guam, which is now a United States protectorate, and apparently is close enough to Asia to be of use in taking care of any trouble. Logical, I think, by any measure.

A hearing was held in April on the movement, with military leaders testifying before the Congressional Committee. A congressman from Georgia, Hank Johnson, said he was concerned about the small size of the island of Guam. He told the officer he thought if all the people on the island were to gather on one side, the island would tip over and everyone would spill into the Pacific.

I really didn't believe it, but my friend told me to Google Guam, and I would find proof.

I did, and there it was, the full interrogation, the congressman carefully explaining his version of the problem and asking over and over, "Wouldn't Guam tip over if too many people were there?"

The Naval officer took a breath, and said that was not a concern, really. But politely told the congressman the Navy would supply him with any geographic information he desired about Guam.

I know geography is not the most popular subject in our schools, and physics is attractive to a limited few. But the congressman from Georgia is a very good argument for improvement in our curriculum.

Go Google Guam. You'll learn something.

I'm Walter Furley, and that is how I see it.

South Texas Fall

7 November 2010

I'm Walter Furley, and this is how I see it.

Fall is here, though most of us in South Texas feel as though it is still summer. The folks who have moved here from up north say they miss those fall seasons in the north, especially in New England.

I've only seen pictures of the forests there turning yellow, orange, gold, and red, with some evergreens mixed in. It all makes a beautiful picture.

My Chinese tallow turns those colors. It seems to do it one leaf at a time, however, and I have to appreciate the colors as they lie on the ground. We do have the rain trees that burst out in a cinnamon color for a few weeks before they drop their leaves. And if we really want to see the northern type of fall, we can drive to the Lost Maples Park in Central Texas.

But all that nostalgia for a New England fall dissipates when winter comes roaring in right behind. The below freezing temperatures, the six feet of snow, the shoveling of the driveways all lessen the attraction of living up north to my mind. Look at all the Snowbirds who like to spend the winter with us. They cite that winter weather as the very reason, even though they say they do miss the turning of the leaves.

Our fall season means just a little change in the weather, permitting some long sleeves if not a jacket or sweater. But it means enormous activity of our football teams and pep squads, and many say fishing is best in the fall. And then there are the fall hunting seasons.

But best of all, our fall weather can't be beat—not too hot, not too cold. As Goldilocks says, "It is just right." And a lot of people agree. The Sunbelt is the fastest growing area of the United States, and Texas is right in the middle of it. It's a very good place to be nostalgic about the fall season up north.

I'm Walter Furley, and that is how I see it.

Holiday Food

30 November 2010

I'm Walter Furley, and this is how I see it.

I've been consuming my share of holiday food and am amazed at how different it is at each dinner at friends and family's homes.

Some are into gourmet cooking, so that nothing is traditional but has an extra something added to make it special. I had never had pumpkin pie with garlic in it but found it delicious. Some Thanksgiving turkeys were stuffed with white bread dressing, which I found mushy compared to my mother's cornbread dressing. And spices new to me were added in most cases. Growing up, I remember sage and thyme in sausage only, never in turkey dressing.

But I liked it that way. The green bean casserole remained consistent, canned beans with mushroom soup and canned onion rings around the top. At every holiday meal, the bean dish was the first to be emptied. Cranberry sauce, I thought, came only from a can, and was served like a jelly. But every meal this year featured homemade cranberry sauce with whole cranberries. Some sauces included orange rind (the cook called it "orange zest"), some with bits of pineapple, and one even added some ginger. It all went well with the turkey. And the turkey! One meal had fried turkey—it tasted like fried chicken. One turkey had been slow cooked all night; others baked in a bag for several hours, and the cooks debated the merits of fresh or frozen birds. Every turkey tasted great to me.

And the gravy! Rich and thick poured generously over the slices of turkey and dressing with a great salty taste that brought back memories of wonderful family meals of the past.

Turkey is the star of Thanksgiving dinner, but my family seemed to have it also at Christmas, indeed almost the same meal.

The holiday food at home with the family is one great thing to be thankful for and to look forward to.

'Tis the season to be merry—the season of the turkey.

I'm Walter Furley, and this is how I see it.

Prejudice

30 November 2010

I'm Walter Furley, and this is how I see it.

I don't like to say it, but I am prejudiced.

When I see anyone with a tattoo or body piercing, I have a real problem with relating to them. My career in reporting television news exposed me to any number of people apprehended by the police, people who had numerous tattoos and many body piercings. The people were arrested for a variety of crimes, some petty, some heinous, but all with most vivid tattoos and disturbing bits of metal fixed on their nose, their lips, even their tongue. It is very difficult for me to separate those enhancements from the criminal type.

I know, some perfectly wonderful people, especially young people, have some artistic tattoos, and some very beautiful girls have a silver ball pierced in their eyebrows, but these disfigurements do not make them more attractive in my opinion. I'm sure they are not seeking my opinion when they have the work done, and they know there are those who *do* find it an attraction.

But as a manager of a newsroom, I could never hire anyone so decorated to represent my TV station in public.

To me the idea reeks of self absorption, and while self improvement and looking one's best is an attribute, tattooing and body piercing do not achieve that goal. The practice indicates such people are much more interested in themselves than in performing any work you might hire them to do.

I find it ironic that many of those people arrested for some of the worst crimes wear religious symbols on their bodies. They obviously do not know the significance of that ornate cross on their bicep or the Virgin Mary tattooed on their chest.

I am trying to overcome this revulsion, however. A lovely young girl waited on me at a store recently, and I was admiring what I thought was a long sleeved blouse on her arm. On a closer look, I saw it was an elaborate tattoo covering her arms from her wrist to her short sleeves. I was stunned. She was already very pretty and did not need that addition, but there it was.

I'm trying, very hard, to see that perfectly good people *can* have tattoos, even body piercing, and still be perfectly good people.

I just wish they didn't make it so difficult to like them.

I'm Walter Furley, and that is how I see it.

Starfish

30 November 2010

I am Walter Furley, and this is how I see it.

I confess to a weakness for writing poetry. Well, not poetry in the sense of Wordsworth, but rhyming verses, sometimes called "doggerel." It's fun, and I even tried to publish some, but they were all rejected. So I'm taking advantage of this time on KEDT to put some of it before the public, so be hereby warned.

I wrote a series of lyrics about sea animals, thinking they would fascinate all who live nearby. But so far…

This one is about the starfish, a subject I doubt has ever been celebrated in rhyme before.

Of all the things that I have seen,
The strangest thing by far:
An odd and most astounding fish
That's shaped just like a star.
It has five arms with pointed ends
That help it crawl on by.
Two point out, two point down
And one points straight up high.
And at the tip of every arm
The starfish has an eye.
That's how it sees to slink away
From sharks that come nearby.
But if a shark should wander by
And eat an arm for fun,
The starfish simply runs and hides
And grows another one.
Now I think it's very smart
To grow an arm again;
Especially when you learn
The starfish has no brain.
The starfish has a spiny top
That's sharp and rough to touch
And underneath are many feet
That help him move and such.
And on each foot, a strange device:

A sucker, very strong,
That lets him fasten tight on rocks
And stay there very long.
Its suckers let it catch its food.
Its mouth and teeth work well
On things like oysters, clams and such.
It bites right through the shell.
A starfish stomach is so strange!
It doesn't keep it in.
It pokes it out to catch its food
Then sucks it back again.
The starfish really's not a fish.
That's not the proper term.
Because it has no bones inside,
It's an echinoderm.
So "Sea Star" is a better name,
Or so some people say.
But I think I will always call
It "starfish" anyway.

There! I've done it. My poems may never be published, but at least one was on the radio, KEDT.

I'm Walter Furley, and that is how I see it.

Caroling

23 December 2010

I'm Walter Furley, and this is how I see it.

I went caroling this Christmas season. A good friend, Beth Hoekje, has organized a group to sing carols in hospitals for the last thirty years or so, and I was allowed to participate in the last several years.

Beth Hoekje is a music teacher and has taught all forms of music including voice, so it is logical she would gather some of her students and performers she had worked with in schools, church, or Harbor Playhouse and lead them in choruses through hospital halls.

The event is invigorating to all of us who participate, but the purpose of course was to brighten the season for others. Beth asked specifically for the oncology wards where many were fighting cancer. We sometimes sang too exuberantly on "Hark the Herald Angels Sing" or "Joy to the World," and one time a nurse asked us to please sing softer because she couldn't hear on the telephone. But the enthusiasm brought many patients to their doors, and others called out for us to enter their room and sing.

I must admit our singing was very good, with some singers music teachers themselves or professional vocalists. And the sound permeated the entire floor. Patients who had been lost in their concerns and worries suddenly were made to think of other things, music, singing, Christmases of their own with all the attendant memories. We were invited into one room where an elderly lady was said to very ill. She smiled weakly at us and asked for "Silent Night," which we sang appropriately. Then on impulse we sang it again using the German words in our choir book. The lady responded by trying to sit up and sing with us. She told us she had come here from Germany and rarely heard it as "Stille Nacht." She was weeping and smiling at us as we sang.

Over the years there have been many such responses. Nurses have written about the affect of the caroling in the hospitals. I, like many in the group, participate each year because it is such an enjoyable, even inspiring experience. And there is the satisfaction of knowing you personally spread some cheerful sounds to those who desperately needed to hear them. I advise it to all. It's the perfect way to take on the Christmas spirit.

I'm Walter Furley, and that is how I see it.

Harbor Playhouse

30 December 2010

I'm Walter Furley, and this is how I see it.

I believe our Harbor Playhouse has arrived at a firm professional standing. I say this after having seen several productions that were first rate, equal to road company shows for which I paid much higher prices than those charged by the Playhouse.

The most obvious improvement in the Playhouse is the technical part of the productions. Scenery is very inventive, lighting is spot on, as they say, and the sound system is so good you forget it is there.

Direction has shown great imagination in stage movement and pacing, with every scene within the shows building to the climax of the production. The choreography for the musicals was astounding for a community theater—imaginative, very physical, in some cases really acrobatic, but always very well done. What is really surprising and pleasing is the fact that there are so many capable dancers in the area to bring these musicals to life. The music in the shows has used both live performers and prerecorded scores but in each case very satisfactory. The theater obviously has a very capable staff to produce the shows.

Most gratifying though is the wellspring of talent available to perform at the Harbor Playhouse. There have been performances approaching anything you see on Broadway. Indeed some cast members have been professional actors. With its emphasis on musicals Harbor Playhouse is extremely fortunate to have so many good singers.

Perhaps we are in a very fortunate wellspring of talent, but there have been years in the Playhouse when talented people were not attracted to its stage because of less than satisfactory productions.

Now, every show seems to be top notch. I was first bowled over by the production of *Cats*, which most people would have called impossible for community theater, then *My Fair Lady*, then *Chicago* (another impossibility), and most recently "*A Christmas Carol*," which I tried to avoid, but with so many friends performing in it, I couldn't miss it. Again, a professional production.

The Playhouse is selling season tickets to the 2011 season. At this point, it looks like a sure thing, a quality season to look forward to.

The Coastal Bend has a theater it can really be proud of.

I'm Walter Furley, and that's how I see it.

2011

2011 Freeze

2 February 2011

I'm Walter Furley, and this is how I see it.

The hard freeze that hit the Coastal Bend this year took away some my prized plants. Most were succulents that needed more protection that the covering I gave them. The esperanza will likely come back with its golden trumpet blossoms, and the hibiscus plant needed cutting back anyway. My neighbor's angel trumpet shrub looks defeated, however, as do the leaves on my aspidistra plants and kalanchoes.

We here in the subtropics we are spoiled with good weather year round. Even hurricanes rarely damage the decorative plants, though they wreak havoc on our beloved trees. But good weather means good growth, and that good growth can get out of hand very quickly. A good gardener is on guard with clippers at all times to keep those shrubs and flowers under control.

But I do not claim to be a good gardener. A vine on my back wall began with pretty little ivy leaves decorating the place, but has grown into a wild, bushy jungle covering the entire wall. I looked a few days ago and some of those vines have become tree trunks that will take a chain saw to be removed. Unfortunately the vine appears to be impervious to freezing weather. If only it had been a casualty instead of the treasured flowering plants.

There's a lesson here somewhere. If you don't carefully tend the plants in your care, they either grow wild or die.

I think my mother said something like that to me years ago, but she was not talking about plants. She was talking about children. And she carefully tended those in her care. Her plants were beautiful, too.

I'm Walter Furley, and that is how I see it.

Church

2 February 2011

I'm Walter Furley, and this is how I see it.

Churches today are going through many changes. And that includes my church. The church services my father grew up with, the church services I grew up with are not attracting the large congregations they once did. And most of us still attending are gray-headed and a little wrinkled.

My church, like many others, has tried to modernize the service with what is called a "Praise Service" which seems to involve the congregation more in the presentation. The music seems to be simpler with few of the old hymns that are a real part of the nation's religious history. Instead simple phrases are repeated over and over like a chant to a simple tune that is always sung in unison. Gone is the magnificent pipe organ, and in its place are guitars, drums, a keyboard of some kind, and lots of microphones. The services such as I have attended are almost mesmerizing with frequent group responses, raising of arms to wave in rhythm with the music. The singers, who are really very good, sound like the popular singers of today, and indeed the whole atmosphere reminds me of a rock concert, much quieter but just as entertaining.

I found myself resisting it altogether. I wanted hymns with a familiar melody with words that fit the meter and lines that rhymed like good poetry. I wanted that full support of the pipe organ swelling toward the climax of the hymn leaving the sanctuary ringing with an echo that could easily be divine. I wanted to hear scripture read sonorously and a sermon that applied it to our present lives.

The praise services are attracting many more people, especially young ones, than the traditional services, which leads me to think I am in error somehow.

And that is likely the case. I drive a car that is twenty years old, but it still runs and serves me well. I have ties and even clothes that I bought at Lichtenstein's forty or more years ago. Some I can even still wear. Even though I have a computer, I still have a fine Royal typewriter which I used for fifty years in the news business.

Change unnerves me. I have loved the things I have lived with these many years and find it hard to relate to the new ways, many of which I find vastly inferior. So time is leaving me behind in the fashionable things.

I can't say I mind. But I worry that our traditions are being trampled, and not replaced with better ones.

I realize this is nothing new. Aristotle complained about the same things. And yet here we are. So bring on the new. I hope you enjoy it as much as I have the old.

I'm Walter Furley, and that is how I see it.

King's Speech

2 February 2011

I'm Walter Furley, and this is how I see it.

I saw a great movie last week, called *The King's Speech.* It had some of my favorite English actors in it, so I thought it would be about the Tudors or the historical monarchs of the land. But it was about a king who reigned in my lifetime, King George VI, the father of the present Queen Elizabeth.

As you likely know by now, the story is about the king's stuttering. He was so badly afflicted, he could hardly finish a sentence without stammering. Apparently he was willing to accept it until his older brother Edward abdicated to marry an American divorcée, shoving young George in line to be King of England. As such, he had to make speeches, and he was terrified at the prospect, especially since a newfangled contraption called "radio" was in use making every sound he uttered into it heard not only by the nation but the world.

So, his wife Queen Mary sought out a speech therapist to help him. The irony is that one expects royalty to do everything better than the rest of us and to learn that the King himself had a serious defect of any kind is astounding.

But there he was, or at least there the actor was. Colin Firth went through rigors of pain to try to speak properly and endured humiliating criticism from his therapist, played by the fabulous Geoffrey Rush. They almost came to blows before the king was almost tricked into speaking without stuttering.

Describing the story now, I see it is really a rather weak one. A man goes to a teacher for speech lessons. Some story. But I tell you, I was on the edge of my seat trying to help the king say his lines and almost giving up hope that he ever would. You remember, it was just after he became king that World War II broke out, and England was threatened with invasion by Hitler. The whole nation and the rest of the world looked to England, and their king, to provide some leadership and reassurance. He had to do by speaking on a live broadcast to be heard around the world. Talk about stage fright. I felt so sorry for the King and the terrible ordeal he faced.

Well, I won't tell you how it ends. But it is a positively therapeutic ending. And I'm reminded of what my parents and my teachers told me over and over again: if you just put your mind to it, you can do anything.

Just as the King did.

I'm Walter Furley, and that is how I see it.

Young Stars

20 February 2011

I'm Walter Furley, and this is how I see it.

I've been intrigued by a young music star that seems to be all over the map right now. Justin Bieber, 16 years old at last count, is selling millions of records, selling out many, many concerts, has been on all the interview shows, and played a role in a top rated crime drama. And just recently he was a guest player on a professional basketball team and hitting baskets with almost every throw. All this happening in just the past year or so. He must think this is the way life is, and isn't it great.

There are several child actors who have had this fame and attention thrust upon them, and so many are in trouble today because they don't know how to handle it. With such adulation they must think they can do anything, and all will be well. Some have been brought down by drugs and alcohol, some by poor driving skills, some for apparent shoplifting or stealing. In all cases, they showed a severe lack of judgment and guidance. They have confused their life of fame with the life that is real. Believing everyone loves and admires them leads them to believe they can do no wrong, and they will be loved and protected anyway.

We parents know young people quite often reject any advice or guidance imposed on them claiming we old folks are just not "with it."

Some of us have learned the hard way that every action we take has consequences, most quite foreseeable. The only thing that saves us is knowing what is right and what is wrong and doing what is right. Parents are supposed to teach us that. If not them, then caring friends. If not them, then the reality of the law will teach them.

I do hope young Justin Bieber will survive this tsunami of fame. I hope he has been taught that achieving in life takes hard work, intense dedication, and the strength to survive failures as well as surviving success. Life for Justin Bieber is very good right now, but still ahead is much more of life, not all of it easy, not all of it good. We wish you the best, Justin.

I'm Walter Furley, and that is how I see it.

Responses

22 February 2011

I'm Walter Furley, and this is how I see it.

Several weeks ago, I expressed my concerns about body tattoos and piercings, explaining that I found them a barrier to my admiring or even liking the persons exhibiting them. Well, several calls from tattoo enthusiasts took exception, one pointing out that many police and fire personnel had tattoos, and they were the ones Mr. Furley expected to protect his property and even his life. I have to admit that in those circumstances, I would never notice nor care whether my protectors had tattoos. I hope I made clear that I did not reject the person wearing the tattoos or piercings, but only the altered body styles. I fear any explanation will not improve my relations with those callers, but I regret offending them, even though tattoos and piercings offend me.

Then a few weeks later I expressed my disdain of the electronic book called the Kindle, and pointed out the pleasure of owning real books attractively displayed on my bookshelves, many of which I happily share with friends and acquaintances. A friend called me personally to tell me how very much she appreciated the Kindle. She said her eyesight was failing, and the Kindle allowed her to increase the size of the print until she could easily read it, and what's more, could press a button and have the book read to her, and press even another button and have it read in either a man's voice or a woman's voice.

Well there is no arguing those merits of the Kindle. She said she had access to hundreds of books and found the Kindle so easy to hold and the bright screen so easy to read. The Kindle is so slim she carries it in her purse and can conveniently enjoy it almost anywhere. When my eyes reach the same condition as hers, and it is appearing that may be soon, I'm sure I'll be happy to own a Kindle. But for now, I still love my books that I've collected over a lifetime, each one recalling a time of my life when I first read it. And even the ones I've lent or given friends (and quite often the loan turns out to be an unplanned gift) I get satisfaction in knowing that inside the cover of that book is my name, and on some of those pages are passages I have marked as especially meaningful or beautiful—a bit of me passed on with my books.

So the ideas I express here are not to change the ideas you or anyone else may have. They are just thoughts that I hope interest you because they interested me, Walter Furley, and that's the way I see it.

TV Spots
23 March 2011

I'm Walter Furley, and this is how I see it.

Since retiring as a KZTV news anchor, I have discovered daytime television, and have become a big fan of "The Price Is Right." The excitement of all that free merchandise just for guessing the right price is irresistible. All the girls displaying the merchandise are real beauties, the emcee is very personable, and every contestant is hyper enthusiastic. It just makes you feel good to watch it all. However, I've noticed the commercials have a grim undertone.

The first one today was for vitamin supplements, a good thing, since vitamins are good for everybody.

Then the next commercial was for an arthritis treatment.

Pain relievers, which are also good.

Then came a spot touting a plan to get your diabetes medicines through the mail. I suppose that is a convenience for those that need it.

Then the next commercial was for a motorized wheelchair, fantastic in its ability to whisk you about with little or no effort.

So I ask myself, how does that show or its advertisers see us in the audience. Undernourished needing vitamins, in pain needing tablets and capsules every day, diabetic with no way to get to the drug store to pick up prescriptions, and disabled to the point of needing an automated wheel chair to get about. But wait, there's more.

The last commercial was for a funeral policy, so your burial could be prepaid when you need it.

The commercials leave me so depressed, I can hardly get excited about all those free new cars, new furniture, fantastic trips all over the world. If I could just see the mute button on my remote, I could edit out the depressing parts and just enjoy the fun parts. But the print on the remote is so small, I often hit the channel changer by mistake and then can't find the show again. Maybe they need a commercial for cheap glasses.

I'm Walter Furley, and that's how I see it.

Black Eye

31 March 2011

I'm Walter Furley, and this is how I see it.

If you have seen me in the last week or so, you may have noticed a very black eye on my face. I don't recall ever having a black eye my whole life, as I am a rather peaceful person and try to avoid situations which could result in a black eye. Cowardice may have something to do with it, but I prefer the term "wisdom."

At any rate, my marred appearance causes looks of curiosity if not concern, and acquaintances always demand an explanation. I hope the others regard me with a certain amount of pity if not understanding and surmise that if I am walking and talking sensibly, I surely must be all right.

But to give the explanation over and over is tiring and even boring. As was the event which caused it.

I walk my little seven-pound dog every morning usually along the very same route, up the block, around the corner, and back again. Well that particular morning I was still slightly sleepy and stumbled on one of our neighborhood cracked sidewalks. The little seven-pound dog was straining at the leash like a dog on the Iditarod team eager to get somewhere immediately, and she exerted just enough force to make me lose my balance and fall on my face. The fall was more embarrassing than painful, but when I put my hand to my forehead, I felt a generous amount of blood. There was blood also on my arm and hands.

As I lay in someone's driveway, my little dog tried to help by generously licking my wounds, which was alarming considering what she had been sniffing in the grass previously. After I got up and resumed the walk, I realized I had pains on my face, my hands, and my side. After getting cleaned up I determined the fall wasn't so bad, but by nightfall a huge purple stain covered my right eye and temple. Little pain but much damage to my appearance. It will remain that way for another week or so, I am advised, so I must endure more and more explanations. One thing I've learned, when I see anyone with a black eye, I'm going to ignore it, just as I hope everyone does when they see mine.

I'm Walter Furley, and that's how I see it.

Spammed

31 March 2011

I'm Walter Furley, and this is how I see it.

I was *spammed* this week! I think that's the right word. I was diligently at my computer reading my email, when I noticed on the inbox a number rising alarmingly fast—75, 76, 77...on up past 90. So I left off reading the mail and clicked onto the inbox, and there were all these messages about undeliverable mail. I had not sent an e-mail in days, but there it was, a page full of undelivered e-mails. Since I am still innocent or ignorant of all the computer machinations, I wasn't sure what was going on. But I began receiving telephone calls from friends who said I had sent them a message offering to sell Viagra! I assured them I did no such thing, and then another friend called to say I had been spammed. Some hacker had gotten hold of all the addresses in my e-mail and sent every one a solicitation to buy Viagra.

I was appalled. I was horribly embarrassed. I was chagrined. I had over 300 addresses in that file, some of which I barely knew but retained just in case. My son advised me to change my password to my email, which I did quickly, but I wonder about all those friends and acquaintances who got the Viagra message. What must they think! I'm hoping they were wise enough to understand what happened, but those whom I barely know must have a definite opinion of a certain Walter Furley. Even worse, my wife and I share the e-mail listings, and her name appeared on the illegal mailings as well. Our good name is likely ruined with many of those 300 people, and we are left with the puzzling questions: who did this, and more puzzlingly, why? Is it possible they are listening to me now, hysterical with laughter at the great success of their prank. I tell you, it's enough to make you go back to writing letters and sending them with a postage stamp. Computers may be a sign of progress, but even progress has its problems.

I'm Walter Furley, and that is how I see it.

Old Radio Shows

9 April 2011

I'm Walter Furley, and this is how I see it.

For some reason, my wife prefers Camay soap over other brands.

However, we cannot find Camay soap anywhere. We find dozens of new brands, all marked new and improved, but not Camay. I remember back when radio was king and television was thought to be impossible, there were many shows sponsored by "Camay, the soap of beautiful women." The commercials were delivered by a voice that sounded like soap for beautiful women. So how could Camay become obsolete? I remember other brands that were so important sounding on the radio: Oxydol on "Oxydol's Own Ma Perkins" one of many fifteen minute serials on each afternoon.

"Pepper Young's Family" with Rinso commercials. And Lifebuoy soap that cured B.O., and I remember the commercial with a fog horn sound that made body odor seem insidiously offensive.

And Cashmere Bouquet soap that sponsored "The Little Theatre Off Times' Square" with Les Tremayne. I think that was on Sunday nights, but Les Tremayne had a heroic voice and always was the perfect lover or hero. I've seen his name on credits in old black and white movies, but I've no idea what he looks like. Then there was Lava soap, which I haven't seen in years, and of course Lux flakes, with "Lux Radio Theatre" hosted by none other than Cecil B. DeMille every Sunday night.

Either I am remembering soap more than anything else, or the advertisers thought we in the audience really needed all that soap. But those brands are now gone so far as I can see. Along with Ipana toothpaste, which I hated but was convinced it was the only one that would do any good. It had to, because it tasted so bad.

It is with a certain nostalgia I recall these products that were so prevalent in the thirties and forties, and I wonder if they are no longer with us because they weren't all that good, or soaps with fancier names just sold better. But they all add up to one thing—nothing lasts for ever. Products we depend on today will likely be replaced by others "new and improved." Just as we who survived the Depression and World War II will be replaced by others who hopefully will also be new and improved.

I'm Walter Furley, and that is how I see it.

Audience

28 April 2011

I'm Walter Furley, and this is how I see it.

We should start public classes to teach people how to behave as an audience. I have had to endure more audience disrespect recently than I feel is acceptable. First of all, people are not being quiet during a performance. That includes cell phones ringing, commentaries to your next seat neighbor, coughing, singing along with the performers, leaving your seat from the middle of the row causing everyone else to stand as you go by... I could go on.

The class would concentrate on instilling a respect for the performers whom you come to hear. That means sitting quietly, listening or watching their exhibition, and then expressing approval with applause or a shouted "bravo," or quietly withholding it if you are not approving.

Boos are for wrestling events.

Hats, especially large ones, are not appropriate in an audience. They invariably block views and defeat their purpose, which is to make the wearer look attractive. I think the person sitting behind someone with a large hat has every right to ask her (or him possibly) to remove it.

I remember in school assemblies, we students were coached rigorously on how to behave, how to set quietly and attentively, and respect those performing on stage. But I have been to symphony concerts where people have wandered around changing seats or looking for friends in the audience. Even young mothers, often in shorts and flaps with two or three children roaming about the auditorium. I remember at one concert, the singer stopped singing and stared frigidly at the woman, who then made her way out of the room. The concert continued peaceably.

A band director told me of a concert in which his star trumpet player played his part in a piece, sat down, and his cell phone rang as the band continued playing the work. And the boy answered it. After a short conversation he turned off the phone and was ready to play his next part of the music.

Afterwards, the director chastised him for it and learned it was his mother in the audience who had called him to tell him how well he did. The director than spoke to the mother, who was outraged that she could not telephone her own son even if he was performing on stage before her.

Audience behavior has deteriorated, just as much of social behavior has deteriorated. Too many think stage performances are the same as football games and behave accordingly. Perhaps a brief lecture before each event asking everyone to please be quiet would help.

But then someone would complain that was hampering their freedom of speech.

I'm Walter Furley, and that is how I see it.

You're Alive

3 November 2011

I'm Walter Furley, and this is how I see it.

I was in my grocery store just the other day, when a rather attractive lady looked at me startled and said, "Walter Furley. You're still alive!"

Well I didn't know what to say, so I laughed. Briefly, but I laughed.

The nice lady went on to say that just today, someone asked her if Walter Furley were still alive, and she said she didn't know, and here she finds me—still alive.

I'm not sure how this has affected me. I am glad to be alive, of course, but to think that someone somewhere thinks I might not be is somehow unnerving.

When I retired from KZTV after 45 years as a news anchorman, I subconsciously wondered if I would lose my identity and become the unknown anchorman. While I was on the air, I grew accustomed to strangers recognizing me, speaking to me usually quite friendly. Then after retirement, there was less and less of that, and I really was not surprised to find that some young people and people new to the city had never heard of Walter Furley and really didn't care to.

But to think that someone thought I had passed away really brought it all home. I was something in the distant past, vaguely remembered like the dinosaurs.

It's likely that the person unsure of my existence is not a KEDT listener, so it would avail little to reassure them on the air that I am indeed still alive.

But I am grateful that the nice lady recognized me and expressed relief that I was indeed still among the living. Perhaps she will spread the word that I am still here and almost as much alive as I once was.

The days do pass quickly at my age, don't they?

I'm Walter Furley, and that is how I see it.

2012

Dog Training

30 January 2012

I'm Walter Furley, and this is how I see it.

It is becoming more and more obvious to me that my dog is training me, instead of the way I planned it.

I have trained her to let us know when she needs to visit outside nature, and the plan was for this to occur each morning upon our mutual arising, then again at night before our mutual retiring.

The problem is she doesn't agree with that schedule, and quite often, always at inconvenient times of day, she informs us of her need to take a walk.

I have given in to adding a noontime visit to the neighborhood, but even that is not enough. And it seems, answering calls of nature is not her objective.

The little dog just likes to take walks. Perhaps she is bored with our sitting watching TV or doing housekeeping or whatever we humans choose to occupy the time. She wants to get out and see the world, the world which I have seen many times before and find less and less interesting.

When she gets her way, she stops her barking and happily permits the installation of her leash, then parades down the sidewalk sniffing out any and all evidence of previous dog visitors. She especially likes to walk past fenced yards where other dogs are living and cause them to bark in protest at her visit to let her know she is trespassing on their territory. She ignores the ruckus, points her nose in the air and trots happily past likely enjoying the attention.

When I feel the outing has reached a satisfying ending, I turn about to return home and find her protesting, pulling at the leash, wanting an even longer walk. There are times when we meet a neighbor, and I stop for a visit of my own only to have her straining at the leash, even barking to get me to keep moving.

And these midday walks rarely produce the activity for which I planned, only a sniffing session leaving me to lead her home from what I call a fruitless mission.

Now it would seem that I, the dog owner, could decide when a dog walk could be permitted, and there have been occasions when I have refused the mid-afternoon sojourns only to find later, that the living room has become her bathroom. So, I am blackmailed (if that's the term) into surrendering to a raucous barking and walking a dog when I would prefer to nap.

There must be an answer to the problem, but then I am still in training. I'm Walter Furley, and that is how I see it.

More Dandelions

30 January 2012

I'm Walter Furley, and this is how I see it.

The dandelions are back. Every morning when I walk my dog, I see new dandelions springing up on the neighborhood lawns, in cracks in the sidewalks, even in cracks in the asphalt in the street. At first, in a burst of altruism or good neighborliness, I pulled them up. The recent rains made it easy, but as the earth grew drier, the dandelions grew stronger and would break off when I pulled at them. And the next morning, the remaining roots would sprout a new dandelion and a stronger dandelion. But they were like the hydra. Each time I pulled up one, two more seemed to grow in its place.

Actually if they would not grow to be so tall and stringy looking, they would be pretty. The first burst of little green leaves and the little yellow flower both look very nice. But they turn into rebellious teenagers and try to cover the entire lawn and multiply by the hundreds. The world could be covered by dandelions, if we did nothing about them. Prolific is too weak a word for them.

I remember as a child seeing them go to seed and form a pretty round bubble of white fur. We would pick them up carefully, then blow on the little ball of white, and make it disappear as thousands of dandelion seeds scattered over the countryside to bedevil us all in perpetuity.

Surely if nature provided such a hardy and plentiful plant, there must be some good in it. Has anyone every tested the leaves or blossoms to see if they contain some marvelous medicinal property? The leaves are likely edible, but certainly not appetizing. Come to think of it, neither is arugula, but we eat it anyway.

Perhaps some chef on the food network could convince us of the healthful benefits of eating dandelion leaves. We would have a plentiful and steady source of new nourishment. There might even be dandelion farms, and field workers would gather the dandelion leaves and put them in those plastic bags and sell them for three dollars each. There's the possibility of a whole new industry that could save the country's economy.

Until then I will keep my weed digger handy and mercilessly rip up by the roots every dandelion in my yard. Now if only all my neighbors would do the same.

I'm Walter Furley, and that is how I see it.

Too Many Books

30 January 2012

I'm Walter Furley, and this how I see it.

I have too many books. Every shelf in my house has books on it, every table, even some of my floor space has books stacked on it. It's an accumulation of over fifty years, if not longer. So periodically I set down to cull out those which I no longer read or want to keep. But I find there aren't any.

Every book was acquired after intensive research or some spur-of-the-moment impulse which I could not resist.

I have a set of leather bound Dickens sent to my grandfather from England, books he treasured, and now I treasure. They are rather small, the size of our present paperbacks, and the print is alarmingly small, but the wine-colored leather with gold imprinting is just too beautiful to ever let go.

Books were a favorite gift as a child, and each one represents the friend or relative who gave it to me. It would be dishonorable to give those away.

In my teen years I was seduced by several book clubs who offered irresistible bonuses when you joined, and of course a new book each month was the latest, and the one the whole world was reading.

One of my favorite bonuses was a complete set of the Will Durant series on the history of civilization. Eleven thick volumes that look so impressive there with the original jackets still on them. They'll stay with me until I die.

During the war (I mean World War II) when paper was very scarce, and few books were published, a book called *Forever Amber* became the rage of the nation. I put my name on the waiting list at the book store and was so excited when it arrived. To save paper, the book was printed in two columns per page, like the Bible is printed. And speaking of the Bible, one book club offered a huge ten-pound edition featuring all the Rembrandt paintings of biblical scenes. The edge of the leaves are brushed with gold, and a beautiful red silk ribbon hangs as a bookmark.

Then I began a collection of Texas history books, many written at the very moment Texas was becoming a state. Descriptions of the Coastal Bend show it to have been extensive plains filled with very tall grass, no mesquite trees or cactus mentioned at all.

Ah, but I must perform surgery on the collection. I am all but drowning in books and must develop a mindset that lets me set them free. So I can make room in my home for more books.

I'm Walter Furley, and I'm a book-aholic. That's how I see it.

Pulling Weeds
27 February 2012

I'm Walter Furley, and this is how I see it.

The recent rains inspired me to inspect my flower garden which has withstood major neglect so far this year. So I should not have been surprised to find more weeds than flowers. I was easily deceived because from my back door the weeds looked like very attractive greenery, in some cases bearing some colorful blossoms. A particularly pernicious weed has long stems with a very pretty blue flower at the end. I've looked it up before and found it is called the Texas Day Flower with two small fragile looking blue petals with a little bright yellow ball at the end of the stamen. I have often thought they would make an attractive hanging basket, though I've never tried it.

Instead I have tried to eliminate it from my garden by pulling it up roots and all. The theory is sound, but each clump of roots is connected to another clump of roots with extensions all around. So no matter how hard I pull at it, or how much I pull up, the roots are still there waiting like insidious predators to return and prevail again.

But the little blue flower weed is not the only unwanted plant there. There are fistfuls of clover, at least two different kinds of grass, and others I can't even describe. At first, I was careful to pull up each little green sprout that looked out of place, but after about ten minutes that diligence gave way to grasping and groping at anything green. That, of course meant some flowers were removed by mistake. The garden is a border along the fence and is the perfect place to replant any potted plants we received as gifts. We have received an amaryllis each Christmas so some forty bulbs have been buried in the plot, some of which have survived. We mix in the Easter lilies each year also, anticipating a burst of colorful blooms each spring. But when pulling weeds by the grasping method, it is difficult to distinguish between green weeds and green flower leaves, so we will have fewer blooms this year.

Weeding the garden made me think that growing a garden was like raising children. You have all these plans for each bulb and see only the beautiful blossom as you set it in the mud, only to have it attacked by weeds and bugs and other unwanted influences that could smother the bulb and leave you with a bed of unsightly green growths.. You have to tend the garden every day to catch the interlopers just the way you have to look after children. And they, like everything else that is worthwhile, require constant attention and loving care. But on a lovely spring morning or on graduation day, you know it's all worth it.

I'm Walter Furley, and that is how I see it.

Possum

9 March 2012

I'm Walter Furley, and this is how I see it.

I caught a possum last week. Now I am no hunter, but my success at the capture gave me a brief sense of accomplishment. We had seen it a few times on our patio, but it was very quick to disappear before we could attack it with a broom or the swimming pool net. Our dog would often wake us up in the midnight hour barking furiously through the patio door at something we could not see, but surmised it was the possum finishing up some left over pet food.

My neighbor had successfully caught several possums with a borrowed city trap. He lent it to me, and I set it up in my garage baited with cat food and looked each morning to see if the trap were sprung. Two days went by, and then the third morning there it was. A medium-sized possum staring at me through the metal bars of the cage. I notified the Animal Control of my success and was told to place the possum in the trap on the curb for pickup the next day.

We did that, but looked at the poor animal several times thinking perhaps we should feed it or put water inside, but there was the possibility that opening the trap would let him escape, so we let him be. The city kept its promise and picked up the possum, but left us the trap. So all seemed to go very well as planned.

But then, a few days later we went into the garage and were immediately covered in fleas.

It was appalling. Hundreds of little black specks jumping on my trousers ready to suck my blood and leave me covered in itching bites. The possum was gone, but his fleas remained. Well, we put the garage off limits immediately and called an exterminator. Without caring if the poison was polluting the earth or not, we wanted those fleas gone and asked him to soak the garage with pesticide. He did so and assured us it was not polluting and was not a danger to outside pets. Fine. Except two days later, as I entered the garage, I was again attacked by a horde of fleas, hopping around on my white trousers by the hundreds. Back to the exterminator. He explained that fleas hatch out every two weeks or so, and we likely had another round of them still ahead. He kindly reinforced the original treatment, and tried to reassure me by saying there was an intense flea infestation all over the city due to the drought, which is difficult to understand, but he knows his business, I'm sure.

So it appears we can't use our garage for another week or so. But I can't help but wonder if I had just let that possum leave on its own accord, and take all his fleas with him, would I have avoided all this trauma.

I'm Walter Furley, and that is how I see it.

Return from Korea
16 March 2012

I'm Walter Furley, and this is the way I see it.

I saw a news story this week that told of a community that organized a welcoming committee for every returning military veteran. As a group they met the veterans at the airport with balloons and flowers and often with other veterans who welcomed them with salutes and families who welcomed them with hugs and kisses. It was very moving to see the scenes, even though you knew the media had been alerted to cover it. The emotions were still real.

I remember back in October 1952 when I was released from the Army after serving in Korea. The troop ship docked in Seattle. Wearing our dress uniforms, duffel bags on our shoulders, we marched onto the waiting buses to take us to the military base for our separation. We were all elated at being home of course and couldn't look hard enough at the Seattle landscape of hills, tall trees, and lots of rain. We were confused by the crowds of people standing on every street in the rain with umbrellas waving flags and cheering.

We wondered who in the world they were waiting for and thought perhaps some high ranking official was about to arrive. We asked the driver what was going on and were visibly shocked at what he said. "They are cheering for you guys. Welcome home."

All the joking and laughing that had been going on ceased immediately. And we stared in wonder at the many, many people waving at the lines of buses carrying us home from Korea. Each one of us felt just as I did, why? What had we done to be celebrated in such a manner. Most of us had been drafted and would never have gone to Korea otherwise. We all did as we were trained, to fight the enemy. We knew buddies who were wounded and wore Purple Hearts. But many of us were coming home because our duties were in a support group, in the motor pool, or even cooks. Some like me were pulled out of the fighting units because typists were needed in the rear headquarters.

I felt like calling out, "No, no, no, don't celebrate us. We didn't do anything. So many of our buddies were not coming home because they actually faced the enemy and died doing it. Celebrate them. Celebrate them."

Even so, it is such a joy to see today's veterans returning. Even one coming home is a victory and deserves celebration and thanksgiving. And each safe return reminds us of what is required to keep freedom alive. We, who now can only watch and pray, can share the joy of seeing the veterans, even though they may feel embarrassed and wonder what is all this fuss about.

I'm Walter Furley, and that is how I see it.

Clothes and Mind

3 April 2012

I'm Walter Furley, and this is how I see it.

There was a fascinating article in the *New York Times* recently which said what you wear can affect your mind and the way you think. I've always thought this, and I feel quite vindicated.

An experiment by scientists placed a white coat on some people who were told it was a coat doctors wear. The very same coat was placed on another group which was told it was a painters coat. Then the people being tested were given a set of two pictures, each very much the same but with several subtle differences. Those in the "doctor's" coats detected nearly all the differences, while those in the "painter's" coats saw very few differences. The scientists concluded that the doctors group saw themselves as intelligent doctors and thus were more alert and quick. The painter coat group felt nothing out of the ordinary and made little effort to examine the pictures closely.

The scientists suggest the way we dress directly affects our behavior and also affects the way others see us.

There are other aspects in the study. People seen holding a warm drink were perceived as warm-hearted people; those with iced drinks were judged cold and aloof. And people carrying a heavy clipboard were judged very important. And research shows that women who dress in a masculine fashion during a job interview are more likely to be hired, and a teaching assistant who wears formal clothes like a suit and tie or nice dress is perceived as more intelligent than those who dress casually.

When growing up, most of us were told we must look nice going out in public, to look neat and clean. That was to give a good impression of ourselves. This new experiment suggests that by looking neat and clean you hold yourself in higher esteem and exhibit better behavior. To quote the article, "Clothes invade the body and brain, putting the wearer into a different psychological state." That's the positive view. The negative view, when you go out in public dressed slovenly in a wrinkled T-shirt and ragged shorts, you indicate your lack of concern about how you look and lack of concern about what others think of you. The implication is: if you dress slovenly, you will act slovenly and behave in an antisocial manner. But if you dress neatly and appropriately, you will behave in a friendly manner and interact well with your fellow men.

I like this theory. It supports what we've known all along—clothes make the man.

I'm Walter Furley, and that is how I see it.

First Grade Foto

19 April 2012

I'm Walter Furley, and this is how I see it.

A friend, who knew where I was born, gave me a book about the history of Marble Falls, Texas, filled with pictures of the town dating from the late nineteenth century to the early forties. There really is an outcropping of marble in the Colorado River there, and water flowed over it authenticating the name of Marble Falls. Things have changed since then, most obviously with the damming of the river and creation of LBJ Lake. Where there once was open pasture land by the river, there are now several communities of luxury homes. Marble Falls was a town of about 3,000, mostly farmers and ranchers or merchants who supplied the community with food and other necessities. Now, the world has discovered the picturesque river banks, the rolling hills, and a lot of very nice people, so that the city is no longer populated with dirt-poor landowners but millionaire residents with eye-popping mansions.

The history book has many pictures of the people and the town from the late 1800s to the fifties, many of whom I can recall easily: the Burnhams, the Giesekies, the Lacys, the Metzgers, the Phinneys—many more names that I recall in my childhood. But the big surprise was: my picture was in the book. Someone had taken a photo of the first grade class of 1936, and there I was along with children I played with and miraculously remember their names: Doug Michel, Sonny Taylor, George Wagenfeuhr, Virginia Ruth Mauldin, Alice Ruth Burnham. I can't help but wonder where they all are now, and if they have changed as much as I have.

I know now that almost everyone was poor by today's standards. My family lived on a small farm with cows, chickens, and pigs, all which were vital food sources. We also had a large garden that grew just about every vegetable known at the time: huge tomatoes, Kentucky Wonder string beans, English peas, several kinds of squash, cucumbers, onions. And what we didn't eat fresh from the garden, we preserved in Mason jars. There were pictures of big peach orchards, plum trees, watermelon, and cantaloupe fields. If we were poor, it was only because we had little money. But the garden we worked so hard to keep growing is paved over now and is the site of a trailer park.

The one street in town that housed the drug store, the theater, the grocery store, The Toggery Shop with men's clothing, and Mrs. Hearn's Ladies Ready-to-Wear, the street that was the life of the town is now the site of new looking buildings, boutiques, real estate offices, even an espresso coffee shop. The Marble Falls I knew is gone, of course, and the new one is much more exciting to visit. But this picture book of *my* Marble Falls, helps preserve what was a happy time in my life. And I am so glad someone had the inspiration, talent, and resources to publish it. Old times have many good times among them

I'm Walter Furley, and that is how I see it.

Mike Wallace

23 April 2012

I'm Walter Furley, and this is how I see it.

I was saddened to read of the recent death of newsman Mike Wallace.

I worked with him in New York back in 1956 and 57. He was the co-anchor of a radio show called "Weekday" along with Margaret Truman. I was the assistant producer, which means I coordinated all the elements of the show and helped make any changes on the air. Margaret was the star, as far as I was concerned. She was the daughter of an ex-president.

Mike was known in New York for an interview show he did on an independent station there. But he quickly became the dominant voice of "Weekday." The program was a last effort of NBC radio to keep its affiliates, which were all defecting from the network and going independent with music, news, and sports. Running from 10:00 AM to 4:00 PM, "Weekday" had a fascinating feature, Meredith Wilson doing a music appreciation segment each day, anthropologist Margaret Mead doing a class on how humans evolved all over the world, a best-selling novel was dramatized in segments for a whole month, and celebrities or news makers were interviewed live in the studio.

Mike was especially good at that, and often elicited some comments from politicians that made the news. Margaret was best at entertainment features and talks with famous people whom she knew. She was very wary of Mike, however who liked to tease her about some of her dad's remarks, like the time he wrote a letter attacking a music critic who had covered a concert she performed in Washington calling her voice a good "church voice." Any comment about Harry S. Truman, and she would get up and leave the studio even while the show was still on the air. Mike knew this and would try often to steer the conversation to something about Pres. Truman.

There were guest hosts who filled in when Margaret was away, one of which was a New York talk show hostess named Virginia Graham. She tended to talk about the more sensational and personal subjects, and revealed that she had undergone an operation that left her incontinent resulting in her losing control if she laughed too hard. Mike loved to tell jokes during the commercial breaks and quite often made Virginia laugh so hard, she would wet herself. And one day this occurred leaving a little puddle under the chair just when a tour was passing through the NBC studios. Mike helpfully pointed out the puddle on the floor as the tourists looked on wondering what it was all about.

But Mike Wallace was dead serious about his interviews and in 1956 was perfecting the technique that he later used on "Sixty Minutes" to great acclaim. He was difficult to work with and often demanded some changes in the scripts which were really unnecessary and did not hesitate to reprimand us underlings if he thought we were underperforming.

He was a dominant presence, however, and made sure everyone in the room knew he was present. Looking back, I realize I enjoyed working with him and see now he was the perfect radio partner for Margaret Truman, making her appear the great lady, and he the stern professional. His technique proved to be very successful. And I, along with many, admire his work.

I'm Walter Furley, and this is how I see it.

Corpus Christi Name

8 March 2012

I'm Walter Furley, and this is how I see it.

Here we go again. I've pontificated on this subject before, but though I see it is doing little good, I must continue my crusade.

It is quite irritating to hear people refer to our city as "Corpus." Our city is named "Corpus Christi," a beautiful name, easy to say, and actually is a unique name. No other place in the world is named Corpus Christi except for the college in Oxford, England, and that is not a city. We don't say "San" and expect people to think we mean San Francisco or San Antonio, though both of them suffer from name contractions. If the name were translated into English, "Body of Christ," would we shorten it to "Body," which is what we do when we say "Corpus?"

I have noticed TV newspeople, especially weather persons, using "Corpus" quite often, and whether they realize it or not they are legitimizing the error to all their viewers.

I once was on a trip home, when I ran into our former mayor, the late Luther Jones, at the Houston airport. As we were greeting each other, the airline desk clerk announced over the loudspeaker, "The plane to Corpus will be departing at Gate 5." Both mayor Jones and myself bristled and immediately went to the desk and he, in a quite friendly manner, explained that he was the mayor of Corpus Christi, and we preferred it to be called by the full name and not the abbreviation. The lady at the desk looked startled but thanked the mayor for the information and repeated the announcement using the full name of Corpus Christi. I'm sure she will remember the full name, but the job of educating the rest of the world remains unfinished.

I don't think it would be impolite to pleasantly correct anyone who says "Corpus" in your presence. They may think you are overly sensitive, but should you mispronounce their name, they would correct you immediately. So it is the same principle.

I'm Walter Furley, and that is how I see it.

Live Audience

23 May 2012

I'm Walter Furley, and this is how I see it.

I attended one of the Metropolitan HD live broadcasts this spring and was completely mesmerized by Anna Nebtremko with a fantastic passage starting at the very bottom of the scale, full volume, then rising to the very top, effortlessly holding that top note so softly I had to strain to hear, then rising to another crescendo—all apparently without renewing her breath. I couldn't help but burst into applause as did several of those in the audience around me, while at the Met in New York, of course, the crowd went wild. Then we in the theater realized they couldn't hear us. We were just spectators.

So I am reminded of the pleasures of going to a live performance. The actors deliver their lines. We laugh, we applaud, and the pacing picks up as the actors realized they are getting through to us. And we become the greatest part of the show. No matter how well a song is sung, how well a dance step is performed, how well an orchestra plays, if it is not heard and appreciated, it is gone forever with the performers wondering if they really did their job.

That's why I think it is so important to support our local music groups. I have seen astounding performances at A&M CC, at Del Mar College, The Aurora Playhouse, Harbor Playhouse, even productions at area high schools are surprisingly good.

And compared to movie prices very inexpensive, yet surprisingly expensive to produce. The theaters, the symphony, the chamber music groups all depend on audience participation to survive, and even then extra special gifts to keep the enterprise going.

This week, Harbor Playhouse is presenting *Sound of Music,* and while it is almost a sing along with everyone knowing all the music, it is still invigorating to see Maria, the children, the Nuns, the Captain all work together to escape the Nazis, and let us applaud vigorously their sincere and earnest efforts to tell you the story. I urge you to go. I urge you to go to every group's performances. You'll be greatly entertained by their efforts and inspired by their talents. And they will be inspired by you, all in a wonderful place, live, right before your eyes.

I'm Walter Furley, and that's way I see it.

Slop Jar
2 June 2012

I'm Walter Furley, and this is how I see it.

A fascinating book was given to me recently, one of the best I've ever read.

It is titled *At Home*, written by Bill Bryson, a man from Iowa, who now lives in England.

He sets the work in an old English home, and then with scientific detail tells how we came to build our houses the way we do, starting with prehistoric discoveries and continuing up the present.

Up until the 19th century, houses anywhere did not contain an indoor kitchen. It was built apart from the main house to avoid the possibility of burning down the whole house. Bill Bryson says the house evolved from one huge room in ancient times to special chambers for the head of the house, some for sleeping, some for special gatherings like a parlor.

Kings' castles of course led the way of home construction. Castles required huge meeting places, like the kings hall, and huge places for dining like the banquet room. And most homes required both a dining room and a living room, but Bryson points out that today many homes have neither, preferring a large family room.

Of particular interest to me was the way houses were built and run in the late 19th century, the Victorian Era. The KEDT-TV series "Downton Abbey" was a perfect example. The wealthy of England, and likely the world, required lavish homes and an army of servants to manage them. Lavish as the homes were, however, there were no inside toilets. Each bedchamber was fitted with a chamber pot and each morning, the servants were required to take the pots from the upstairs chambers down to a place far outside for disposal.

This particularly interested me, because I grew up in the early thirties in Marble Falls, Texas, on a small farm with a modest home having *no* indoor toilet. Everyone on our side of town had a privy or an outhouse. So, any nighttime requirements were met with a chamber pot. We children preferred the term "slop jar." And one of my childhood duties to empty the chamber pots or slop jars each morning.

I really thought nothing of it, though I'm sure I protested, but that was the routine of all homes out in the country just like those in England it turned out.

Well, in 1953, I visited my cousins in England, partly to celebrate getting out of the Army and partly to accompany my 85 year old Auntie on her first trip to Texas. On my arrival in London Auntie served me a beautiful English tea, in her favorite tea set made by Wedgewood, a beautiful shade of blue with white overlay of classic designs called "jasper ware." The teapot was exquisite, sugar bowl a beauty, a cream jug perfectly designed. There was another large, empty bowl. And as Auntie emptied the dregs of her cup into it, I asked what that bowl was called. "Oh," said elegant Auntie. "That's the slop jar."

I'm Walter Furley, and that is how I see it.

Fruit Plates

18 June 2012

I'm Walter Furley, and this is how I see it.

I know I must have a reputation for griping, especially of little things.

But little things grow into big things, and one little thing can spoil one very big but wonderful thing.

I am thinking of the fruit cup that often comes with restaurant meals: usually very pretty with green melon, cantaloupe, golden pineapple, blueberries, red strawberries, green kiwi fruit, always looks delicious.

Until you bite into the green melon slice and find it unripe, hard, and tasteless. The same with the cantaloupe. Even the strawberries have a dense white center instead of a rich, red one. And the pineapple has to be that Golden Pineapple, or it is just a waste of time.

I know how difficult it is to pick out perfectly ripe melons or even strawberries, but I am not a restaurant chef. If I am to be charged for a fruit cup what a whole pound of the fresh fruit itself costs, that fruit ought to taste the very best. And too often it doesn't.

Were I the chef, I would insist the fruit cup preparer taste every melon or fruit before putting it out for customers to assure him and us all that it is really good and worth that extra charge.

I'm Walter Furley, and that's the way I see it.

Saving Europe

18 June 2012

I'm Walter Furley, and this is how I see it.

I came across an old booklet recently entitled "Citizen's Food Committee" and was ready to toss it out when I decided to examine it more. It was the fascinating story of how we Americans saved Europe from starving after World War II.

All of Europe was severely damaged by the bombing. Farmlands were rendered useless by bomb craters, to say nothing of buried bombs. Food factories were destroyed. There was just no source of food for those Europeans who survived, so President Truman appointed a man named Charles Luckman to head the Citizen's Food Committee.

First he had to find out how much food America could spare. There had been a bad drought in 1947, so our output was down. But he asked all the food industries how much they could spare. The wheat industry would be a major contributor because Europe had almost no bread. The meat industry found what it produced was barely supplying this country, so Mr. Luckman asked us Americans to cut back on our meat consumption by observing "Meatless Tuesdays." Families would eat no meat on Tuesday; restaurants would not feature meat on Tuesday menus. The slogan was "Save Meat! Save Wheat! Save the Peace!" The committee began organizing all America to support the campaign—newspapers, magazines, famous people making speeches, a pervasive radio campaign. Remember there was no television in 1947.

Well, it worked. From all over the country, special food trains were put together filling each car as it moved from the western farmlands to the eastern seaports. Folks in the south felt neglected, so they formed their own food train and sent even more tons of food to be taken to Europe.

Besides Meatless Tuesdays, there were Eggless Thursdays, and Americans were asked to limit their bread intake to only one slice a day.

Well, the plan worked. Not only was the food provided the starving of Europe, but Americans learned how to be proficient in producing food itself. It found cattle and chickens could be produced with far less grain feed than used, and Americans needed to cut back on their own food consumption anyway.

Isn't that a great story?

Makes you wonder what would have happened if we had done that after World War I, instead of just letting Europe stew in the problems of their own making, which made Europe so angry and vengeful they brought us World War II.

And what about America today? The homeless, the starving, the people living on the streets with no way care for themselves. Should we have another national food committee?

Local food banks would like the help, I'm sure. Actually, in Africa and other parts of the world, the food shortage is just as critical.

But it is not insurmountable. If we could feed all of Europe by sacrificing in 1947, we can do it again today. All we need is another Harry Truman and Charles Luckman to whip us into shape.

I'm Walter Furley, that is how I see it.

Changing Anthem

2 July 2012

I'm Walter Furley, and this is how I see it.

They are talking about changing our national anthem again.

I read an article the other day that someone somewhere is going to ask Bruce Springsteen to write a new national anthem. Also on the list are Dolly Parton and Brittany Spears, all successful performers and millionaires as a result. But I question their ability to write a moving anthem expressing our deep love of country.

The present anthem is perfect. We don't need a different one. It expresses the danger that faces our freedoms; it expresses the valor of those defending it and expresses the triumphant hope that keeps our country alive.

More than that, I think it expresses the hopes and dreams of those who fought and died to keep this country free. From out of the past this cry comes asking if the country is still free, did thy die in vane? Just listen to the words of the anthem and say them with me. We all should know them by memory.

Oh, say can you see
By the dawn's early light
What so proudly we hailed
At the twilight's last gleaming

These are words of one who died fighting to the last, whether at Concord or Antitem or Pearl Harbor or Battle of the Bulge. They want to know: was it worth it? The last thing they saw likely was the American flag.

Whose broad stripes and bright stars
Through the perilous fight
O'er the ramparts we watched
Were so gallantly streaming?
And the rockets red glare
The bombs bursting in air
Gave proof through the night
That our flag was still there.

Now comes the real gut grabbing part that is aimed directly at you and me.

Oh say does that star spangled banner yet wave
O'er the land of the free and the home of the brave?

Does it still? And are you doing your part to be sure it still waves?

You don't have to be in the military to keep this the land of the free. Do your part to be sure we all have freedom, that we all are united, that we all care for our country, we all care for each other.

This Anthem has contributed so much to our way of expressing our love for our country. It gave us the phrase "Star Spangled Banner," a loving way to speak of our flag. "The land of the free and the home of the brave." That phrase means only one country in this world. The anthem ends with a challenge we must all accept and win:

Oh say does that star spangled banner yet wave
O'er the land of the free and the home of the brave?

We can have no better anthem than that.

I"m Walter Furley, and that is how I see it.

New Bio of Cronkite

12 July 2012

I'm Walter Furley, and this is how I see it.

A friend delighted me with a gift recently of a copy of a new biography of Walter Cronkite. I was surprised to learn of its publication because I thought the man had written his own, and it turned out quite well. The author of the new book, Douglas Brinkley, thought he knew better, and included a lot of material that he thought showed Cronkite to be even more influential in television news that he knew himself. And I think Brinkley has a point.

My main interest, of course, was Cronkite's relationship with my former employer Col. Vann M. Kennedy, the owner of KSIX-AM and KZTV, Channel Ten.

It was a well-known fact the Cronkite's first job was with Col. Kennedy, when both were in Austin, and Cronkite was attending The University of Texas. He served as a reporter for two of Kennedy's weekly newspapers and gathered and reported news under the Colonel's direct supervision.

Cronkite said, and Brinkley repeated, that experience instilled him such an ethic for all news that he patterned his career on what he learned. I personally knew of the Colonel's obsession with getting it right. Every name in a story had to be verified by the phone directory or the city directory, and that meant checking and rechecking every item. Every fact and quote had to be attributed, and notes kept to verify them. When radio and television came into the picture, we had the tapes to prove what we wrote was true. One admonition I'm sure Cronkite heard often, "Write the story as if it were about you and you are innocent."

A perfect example of Cronkite's style was the delivery of the news of the death of President Kennedy. I had heard on one radio station that he had died, but Cronkite stared into that news camera, insisting the reporter on the telephone verify the death report before Cronkite put down the phone, took off his glasses, wiped his eyes, and said it was official the president had died at 11:20, just a few minutes previously.

The new author saw Cronkite more aggressive than we did on TV. He also implied that he betrayed Edward R. Morrow after promising to join his CBS team in Europe during World War II. Cronkite instead joined INS as an independent news reporter and made the reputation with which we are all familiar. Indeed, CBS eventually made Cronkite the molder of CBS news, and in so doing molded all television news as we know it today. He also said Cronkite later resented being retired at age 65, so that Dan Rather could assume top anchor position.

I think many of us could understand that. Whatever anyone writes about Walter Cronkite, they are writing of how TV journalism was born and how it was practiced in its early history. I am not sure the news is still being reported with the Cronkite values today.

I'm Walter Furley, and that is how I see it.

Sold Houses

12 July 2012

I'm Walter Furley, and this is how I see it.

A house in our neighborhood sold recently, and I wondered if the buyer knew that almost forty years ago a husband shot his wife to death there. It's a perfectly good house, well maintained, very attractive and at one time remodeled. I wonder if the seller even knew there had been a murder in the house.

Several of the houses on our street have had tragedy visit them. One young wife was raped as she carried her groceries from the car through the garage. She never reported it, but became almost a recluse afterward, rarely coming out even into the yard. The family moved soon afterward.

Two houses had people who died of natural causes. I remember the ambulances and firetrucks that appeared at the scene.

A young man was killed while cleaning an "unloaded" gun in a house just across the street and down the block. The whole neighborhood was sad.

I doubt if the buyers of these homes, which are very nice ones by the way, thought to ask if anyone had died there. And does it matter? When new owners move in, the house takes on a new life, a new history. No one really cares if "George Washington Slept Here." It's the bottom price that becomes important, whether a new roof is needed. Is the plumbing in good shape?

Every house has a story, just as the historic houses in the east. Some have changed owners so often it would be difficult to remember all that happened, even though most of these homes were built in the 1950s. Few hundred-year-old structures survive in Corpus Christi.

Most of the folks in my neighborhood are retired couples, few children in the immediate vicinity. And as life takes its course, many of these houses will be up for sale. I doubt if any buyer or seller would want to know that people died in their new home. But they also lived, laughed, loved, and tried to be good neighbors to all. As the poet Edgar A. Guest wrote, "It takes a heap of living to make a house a home." These are fine homes on my street.

I'm Walter Furley, and that is how I see it.

Typewriting
13 August 2012

I'm Walter Furley, and this is how I see it.

My handwriting has not improved in my eighty-four years.

I have tried to maintain the Spencerian method taught in Marble Falls Grade School, which encourages students to handwrite the way Thomas Jefferson did in the Declaration of Independence. Good luck with that.

So to ease the efforts of my correspondent's deciphering my message, I decided to use my old Royal typewriter, which I had restored a year ago to new condition.

What a revelation. After using the soft touch computer keyboard with its back spacing and correction features, I found that typewriter keyboard a workout. I could not believe that once in junior high typing class I had attained the stratospheric summit of one hundred words a minute. That I had built a career on typing news stories for my television station, typing them fast to meet deadlines, and typing them well so they could be read easily on the air.

Today, it took every effort to type like that again. Hunt and peck was the only useful method. Even then I made mistakes and had to erase and retype. Do they make whiteout anymore?

So I gave up the idea and went back to the soft touch computer keyboard. I thought about apologizing for not handwriting my message, but thought it would be a little hypercritical.

Then it struck me. I am not alone. All my generation has succumbed to the soft touch computer.

A few maintain a fine handwriting, but eighty-five years can erode that quickly. My signature remains the only thing I bother to write. Taking notes on the telephone I've learned to print, or the note is lost among the Egyptian hieroglyphics.

There was a time when everything was expected to be done with some grace: polite greetings, what you wear in public, table manners, legible handwriting, even well-enunciated speech, personal messages written in personal handwriting. Now minimum effort, anything seems acceptable.

So there it sits. My shiny Royal typewriter, waiting to do its duty, if only I remember how.

I'm Walter Furley, and that's how I see it.

Digital

30 August 2012

I'm Walter Furley, and this is how I see it.

In rummaging through some bureau drawers the other day, I found some film still in its cartridge, never developed. No date on it, but nothing to indicate it was defective. So I had it developed and was delighted to find it was a roll of film taken of me and my two boys when they one and two years old. We were preparing for a Christmas portrait with them laughing and squirming resisting the dress-up procedure. The pictures captured the joy of the moment which here some forty-five years later I could tearfully but happily relive.

We rarely use that camera anymore, a fine 36 millimeter slide camera.

We use our digital. We snap pictures generously, look at them instantly on the camera screen, then put it away, perhaps never to look at them again. I fear I've lost something by giving up film. I always took the roll to a developer who would give me two copies of each print for just a little more, so I could mail copies to family and friends and store the rest to be looked at years from now as I go through overflowing bureau drawers.

I know. You can remove the little black chip from the camera, take it to the developer for processing into prints. You can even put the little black chip in your computer and E-mail it to your developer, who can have the prints ready for you that same day. But I have yet to learn how to do that and may be too stubborn to learn. As you may have surmised from some of my editorials, I resist change and feel very comfortable with the way things have always been.

However, I must admit the film industry has done its part to confuse me.

From the simple Brownie Kodak black and white prints, it went to complicated cameras requiring a knowledge of F-stops, shutter speeds, then to slide cameras and many variations there of, and then the automatic cameras that not only judged the amount of light needed, but focused automatically. I became an expert by just buying the latest model. Yet, I have hundreds of color slides with no way to project them on a screen (which always was a boring chore).

So digital it is now and likely to remain so.

But perhaps years from now, I shall find a little black chip which I can insert in my computer and find a charming moment of my life I have long forgotten and again give thanks for the wonder of photography.

I'm Walter Furley, and that's how I see it.

Perfume

30 August 2012

I'm Walter Furley, and this is how I see it.

While out walking last evening, I caught the drift of a mild perfume where some nice lady had recently walked. It reminded me of a scent my mother used, subtle, barely discernible but pleasant and nice.

It also reminded me of another perfume that I remember distinctly.

During the war I got a summer job at the Naval Air Station as a clerk. This meant I had to carpool every morning at an early 6:00 a.m., five of us crowded in a1940 Chevrolet, three men, my teenage self, and a very attractive lady named Rita, who wore a very strong perfume called "Prince Matchabelli." I know, because I asked her the name. I thought it smelled great, spicy, sweet, heady like a woman ought to smell, and boy, did it linger. I suspect each of us men retained a little Prince as we went our separate ways each work day. Rita was perhaps a little overweight and liked to wear dresses which were cut low in front. It was pleasant to squeeze in beside her with all three of us in the back seat. Remember air conditioning was not available during the war, so not only were the bodies quite close, but so was the air.

Prince Matchabelli was a lasting perfume, because it was just as apparent on the ride home as the ride to work.

I've never come in contact with the Prince since that summer. I remember a bookkeeper in our television station who wore something she called "Tabu," but it wasn't nearly as attractive.

My wife prefers a subtle, gentle scent called "Joy," which smells just like fresh roses. It's expensive, but suits her (and me) perfectly.

I often wonder what happened to Rita and Prince Matchabelli. I used to see it advertised in magazines, a bottle shaped like the royal crown of England with a jewel like knob for the stopper. I wonder if it really smelled the way I remember it. The years may have enhanced its enchantment somewhat.

But it will always conjure up the image of Rita, laughing, giggling, beautiful Rita. Perhaps some night while walking, I will get a whiff of what I remember of Prince Matchabelli and know that Rita has passed this way.

I'm Walter Furley, and that is how I see it.

Jekyl-Hyde

October 2012

I'm Walter Furley and this is how I see it.

Harbor Playhouse continues to amaze me. It's new production of *Jekyll and Hyde* is far above the quality that could be expected of any community theater.

The acting professional, the singing first rate, but it is the production itself that leaves you astounded. Director Joel Earley expertly moves crowds on and off a one set stage, that is transformed magically from a scientist's laboratory, to a hospital, to London streets, to the interior of a London mansion, all by lighting and dropped screens—pure theater. The coordination between stage crew, lighting, and cast is nothing short of perfect, and a very difficult musical is presented almost flawlessly.

Particularly talked about is the performance of the lead, Jake Raper. His bio listed him as a graduate of TAMU-CC, with a major in theater. He must have made all As because his energy and complete absorption of the role was mesmerizing.

The goal of any production is to make the audience forget it is watching a play or musical, but is hearing a fascinating story. And that is what happened at Harbor Playhouse this weekend. The players, the music, the costumes all blended together to get Robert Louis Stevenson's story told. It was a most satisfying evening.

The general output of Harbor Playhouse seems to be at its peak of high quality production. The past several seasons have brought us outstanding performances such as *Cats* and *Chicago* either of which would have seemed beyond the capability of any community theater.

Last year's *Christmas Carol* had many brand new effects that were most effective. The theater seems to be in the hands of a professional staff which is ensuring that every production is presented with a professional polish and certainly worth the support of its community. And the support is rewarding, too; it assures great theater for all the Coastal Bend.

I'm Walter Furley, and that is how I see it.

Violence on TV & Movies

October 2012

I'm Walter Furley, and this is how I see it.

News flash: There is too much violence on television and in the movies.

I remember hearing that when "Gunsmoke" was the big show in TV, but compared to shows today, "Gunsmoke" was a wimp.

Watching a series of shows a few nights ago, I noted each one had several cars blown up by fire bombs, with the vehicle careening in flames across the street, turning over at least twice, leaving several bodies in its wake. Watching previews of movies in the theater, more cars are blown up crashing into others making a conflagration that approaches Armageddon. Huge explosions demolish skyscrapers, and cars come crashing through cement walls and falling several stories down on innocent bystanders—arresting visuals likely costing hundreds of thousands of dollars to fabricate. Even if they are generated by computers, the effect on the screen is still mayhem and violence, as though no good movie or TV show could be made without it.

And in TV crime shows we have become so used to bloody anatomies, extreme closeups of inner body details that the shock value of such scenes leaves us numb and insensitive.

And that in itself is alarming. We should react with horror and disgust at the sight of a mutilated body. Human empathy should make us feel the pain of such a scene, even though what we are seeing is likely a lot of wax, latex, and gallons of red paint. Instead we are all but inured to the depiction, having seen it so many times, we are numbed and blasé to it all.

I wonder if this carries over into real life. So many of the car wrecks seen in the news are too reminiscent of those on TV dramas, especially those involving fire. Do drivers think because they see speeding autos on television, they can also speed like that on our city streets? Do they think because TV script writers conveniently dispose of dead bodies, these wrecks do not involve real, once-living people whose happy lives are forever taken away for no good reason?

Then when the newscasts come on, the violence we've seen in the crime stories have numbed us to the horrible violence we see in the wars in the Middle East.

It seems to me we have come to accept violence—detailed, specific, horrible violence—as just a way of life, even an entertaining way of life. Remember the Romans and the Coliseum? They organized big shows of innocent victims thrown into the Coliseum with wild beasts, or even gladiators who had to fight to the death. How different are we today?

I'm Walter Furley, and that is how I see it.

Women's Fashions

October 2012

I'm Walter Furley, and this is how I see it.

How do you women survive in wearing bare shoulder dresses?

There have been recent days and evenings when I was grateful to wear shirt and jacket, but the women at the event were wearing bare shoulder gowns that made them look especially attractive but with no protection whatever from the chill of the evening.

And the practice is not limited to evening wear.

Beautiful young ladies appear at the malls wearing extremely short shorts with a thin top that is sleeveless and usually cut low in the front. Again, very attractive, but the air conditioned mall or restaurant would seem to make that outfit uncomfortably cool.

I've noticed that the young and beautiful ladies predominate in wearing this minimum fashion. It's the older ones who cover up their shoulders and even wear a light jacket, so I know it is not only we men who feel the coolness of the day or the air conditioning.

Beautiful bare shoulders have always been in high fashion. Look at the art of the last few centuries. While the artists seem to have preferred models who were nude, those in formal wear stood straight and proud showing off their beautifully rounded shoulders. Whistler's *Madame X* wears a classic black dress that stops conveniently to let her throat and shoulders show off to high advantage. The aristocratic women of the Victorian Era all apparently felt they were not properly dressed unless their bare shoulders were exposed.

I don't mean to be griping about the fashion. In fact, I greatly admire it, and thank the women for going through what I would call discomfort to look so fetching and attractive.

But I can't help but wonder, don't they get cold? I shiver for them a little when I see them pass by knowing full well they are getting my attention.

I'm Walter Furley, and this is how I see it.

iPhones

15 November 2012

I'm Walter Furley, and this is how I see it.

There is just too much change, too fast, in this world!

A few Christmases ago I bought my wife an iPhone, a little expensive I thought but found it delighted her so much, I decided it was worth it. First of all the audio was so very loud and clear, it made other phones seem inferior. Then I learned it could contain an entire telephone directory of just the numbers she called most often. What's more, she could scroll one up on the screen, touch a little square, and it was dialed automatically. The subscription plan lets her contact friends in Europe as easily as in town, so easy that she has called some by mistake to their mutual surprise. She can get a weather map on her iPhone; she can get a tuner so she can tune her harp to perfect pitch; she can store recipes on the phone, keep addresses of all her acquaintances, write grocery lists, type in reminders on a calendar, and much more than I even know about.

Frankly the thing intimidates me, if not scares me. When it rings, I invariably touch the wrong square on the screen, and my wife has to return the call with the explanation, "Oh, my husband..."

At any rate, she has conquered the iPhone. She can even take and send pictures on it. And they are of surprisingly good quality. But now I learn that this model phone is going to be obsolete. A new model is already on sale, and an even newer and more improved one is in the future. It's going to take a college night course to learn how to operate the thing.

Remember when a telephone was a telephone. They were all alike, black mostly. You picked up the receiver when it rang, and put it back on the hook when the conversation ended. And we thought we were so advanced from the party lines and weak connections of yesteryear. Have you noticed movies made as late as the 1970s had cradle phones, pay phones, and phones available only on your desk or in a phone booth. What was wrong with all that, that we had to improve it to become a hand-held computer?

Movies and television dramas today couldn't exist without the ubiquitous cell phones. Come to think of it, many of us think we couldn't exist without them either. But with the changes that persist in controlling everything, even cell phones may become obsolete, an amusing toy our grandfathers once used. Frankly I won't mind. Except what will replace them?

I'm Walter Furley, and that's the way I see it.

Sue Finley

15 November 2012

I'm Walter Furley, and this is how I see it.

Del Mar College held the grand opening of is newest building recently. The college named it the Sue Sellers Finley Theatre in honor of the work she did in building up the Drama Department at Del Mar.

In a documentary shown before the opening, we learned of her training in several Texas colleges, her career on the New York stage, and her coming to Corpus Christi when her husband moved here in his job. Sue Finley immediately became active in Little Theatre, both performing and directing. She was gifted in both areas, a consummate performer with the added ability to make others good performers.

So when she took on the job at Del Mar she knew what she had to do and how to do it. Through her efforts the college built the Nell Tribble Bartlett Theatre, a small arena theatre seating about 150. But goals were bigger. Sadly she developed a terminal disease that cut short her plans for Del Mar drama.

But the dream persisted, and her fellow teachers, students, and perhaps more importantly the school itself, raised the money, hired the builders, and produced the excellent building that was opened just recently.

The opening production was *A Funny Thing Happened on the Way to the Forum,* by Stephen Sondheim. It was delightful and showed the great enthusiasm behind it all—the students' performances, the shiny new look of the theatre, the expert lighting system, all shown off proudly by the show and its producers.

The story of the Sue Sellers Finley Theatre is a model one for any project. The goal has to be envisioned by a visionary, and that vision has to be shared and believed in by fellow workers or dreamers. The whole idea, the whole dream has to be kept alive and made the goal of many for it to become a reality. The work that went into financing took hours and very persuasive talking. And all had to be convinced of the need. With that kind of support, with that kind of commitment, most any project or goal can be reached. Our city government, our national government could learn how to work together to bring about the growth and changes we all need.

I'm Walter Furley, and that is how I see it.

Kline Dedication

9 December 2012

I'm Walter Furley, and this is now I see it.

The Corpus Christi Symphony Christmas concert this weekend was delightful. Rich orchestrations of the great Christmas music, a mass choir to sing it, and some soloists who made it even more outstanding.

The concert was dedicated to its past manager, Litta Kline, who died this week.

She managed the orchestra from 1954 to 1994, a full forty years. And they were turbulent years. That was the time when big corporations began to pull out their donations to all the arts, mostly because the tax credits they had enjoyed were being pulled out from under them.

For a time it looked as if the Symphony could not make it. Each concert cost thousands of dollars just for the performers, and there was always the office costs whether there were concerts or not. But Litta Kline knew how to cut corners. She arranged for building owners to give her office space, she begged and borrowed office equipment, and literally made a Symphony office out of nothing.

She personally handled all the contracts for the musicians, still getting the most talented ones available. She worked with the conductors to build a real professional symphony orchestra, and kept it going through some very lean years. That was because she was able to persuade some of the city's businesses to come through with donations in those extreme emergencies.

But the threat was constant. Litta Kline knew if she let down, the Symphony would go down.

When conductor Maurice Peress became director, he wanted to present operas, the most expensive thing an orchestra can do. But he, and later conductor Cornelius Eberhardt, showed Litta how it could be done, and together, they produced *twenty* fully-produced operas, complete with classic sets and costumes. Opera singers from all over the world were eager to participate, and Corpus Christi audiences saw some spectacular performances.

But the orchestra built by Litta Kline had grown so much, that she decided her forty years as manager was enough, and she retired. She had worked with only one assistant. It took five salaried people to replace her.

All the arts in Corpus Christi have been through this all too familiar crisis and through heroic efforts by leaders in the ballet, museum, and theatre fields have survived. But Litta Kline was unique. She was a leader and a worker.

And the combination made our Symphony what it is today.

I'm Walter Furley, and that is how I see it.

Royal Pregnancy

9 December 2012

Our nation's sense of humor is getting out of hand. It is infecting the humor of the rest of the world.

The humor on "Saturday Night Live" is usually witty and satirical and very well-acted, but it can be raucous, tasteless, and even cruel. Witness the recent political campaign. Because the show is successful, it seems to give license to anyone else to be just as mean and cruel in making a joke.

I was made aware of this just recently when two radio disk jockeys in Australia made a prank call to a London hospital where Prince William's wife was ill with the first stages of pregnancy. Apparently the radio personalities made it through to the nurses station attending the Duchess, and was given a private, detailed report on her condition. She was much better, it turned out.

But the nurse at the switchboard who let the call go through was extremely embarrassed and distraught at what she had done. A few days later, her body was found in her apartment, an apparent suicide. It was a tragedy that should never have happened.

And it would not have happened had the disc jockeys held the Royal Family in respect and not invaded their privacy. Prince William must be thinking of the paparazzi and the death of his mother.

But English Royal Family members, like all those in public life, are subject to unfair and often libelous ridicule. That should not be. The satirists and comedians feel protected from such ridicule or may even cultivate it to enhance their careers. But the harm they can do to their subjects is never even considered. Some critics have said the "Saturday Night Live" political skits and the relentless bad jokes about the politicians influenced the outcome of the election. Voters are not going to vote for candidate who is characterized as a joke day after day.

Everything we do or say has consequences. This important fact is rarely considered in media comedy. There is no evidence the performers thought before they spoke. Even inadvertent actions can cause tragedy. Remember when the US military burned some old and damaged Korans? Muslims were so offended, there were riots and killings around the world.

I understand the Australian disk jockeys have been taken off the air, but I doubt the late night comedians will ease up on their attack on anyone they think vulnerable. Frankly such jokes are rarely funny. Let us hope that alone will eventually kill the practice.

I'm Walter Furley, and that is how I see it.

Sleeve Sneezing

28 December 2012

I'm Walter Furley, and this is how I see it.

It's really heartening to see how quickly the American public has accepted the practice of sneezing into the crook of their arm instead of spraying the sneeze into all the world about them. The procedure looks a little odd or different but is apparently effective.

Now if you sneeze into your elbow crook and you are not wearing sleeves, there may be a problem if you have no tissues to use. But at least you have made the effort to protect those around you, and while they may decline to shake your hand, they can at least appreciate your concern for them.

Should you be wearing a warm sweater or a very nice jacket, the sneeze routine seems to me to be sacrificial. Even just one sneeze can make the garment eligible for cleaning or washing, and really, it's much like wiping your nose on your sleeve. It's going a little too far to ruin nice clothing to catch a sneeze.

Before tissues there were handkerchiefs, and in wintertime it was wise to check to see that one was in your pocket at all times. Of course it was used over and over and really became a collector of germs and likely spread or prolonged the cause of the sneeze. But you weren't well-groomed if you had no handkerchief. We were even expected to share it with someone who had none, used or not.

But is it all that difficult to be armed with tissues? Small pocket sizes are available, and if not then wad up a fistful and carry it in your pocket. Most sneezes predict themselves so you can retrieve a tissue from the pocket or purse and catch those dreadful germs that live in sneezes before they convulse your body.

I may sound like one who is against public hygiene. Not so. We should do all we can to keep the world a clean and healthful place, just as we should keep ourselves clean and healthy. But all within reason.

I'm Walter Furley, and this is how I see it.

Spaghetti

28 December 2012

I'm Walter Furley, and this is how I see it.

A television chef showed the greatest way to eat spaghetti I have ever seen. I've always had trouble eating it the Italian way—start winding on a fork, held in place by a spoon, ending up with a wad of spaghetti on the fork that you had to eat like a chicken leg. Very primitive, I think.

Or you can dip the fork into the spaghetti, put the pasta in your mouth and bite off the excess. Of course you have to hold your head right over the plate, or the spaghetti will fall right into your lap always missing the napkin which you have used to wipe away the excess marinara sauce which will not wash out of ties or a very nice shirt.

How else to eat spaghetti? Take a knife and fork and cut it up in your plate. With smaller strands of spaghetti you can successfully get a decent bite into your mouth. But this is the way to serve children, and we grown people prefer an adult method.

Another way is to get the end of a long strand of spaghetti and suck it in until you get it all in your mouth. Another a favorite method used by children. And again one which we adults avoid. The last few inches flay about like a garden hose and leave the red sauce on your face, on the table, and likely on your very nice shirt.

But this chef on TV had what I call the perfect answer. She broke up the Spaghetti before she boiled it, so that the bits measured about two inches, long enough to hold the marinara sauce and of a manageable size to get onto a fork and into your mouth. I realize this method is similar to the one where you cut up the pasta in your plate, but her method eliminates that.

It is puzzling that I have lived all these years and just now figured out how to eat spaghetti. I wonder what else I have not figured out.

I am Walter Furley, and that is how I see it.

Index

Symbols

A

B

C

D

E

N

O

P

R

S

T

U

V

W

Y